FREE MY HEART
OF GRIEF
TO LOVE

A JOURNEY FROM
LOSS TO JOY

A MEMOIR BY
SANDRA MOORE BERNSEN

God's Pure Love, Peace
& Joy to you

3-1-12

Free My Heart of Grief to Love

Borderline Publishing LLC
406 S 3rd Street
Boise ID 83702
www.borderlinepublishing.com

Library of Congress Control Number: 2011942500

ISBN 978-193640846-7 (Paperback)
ISBN 978-193640847-4 (eBook)

I. Title
 2011

This novel is a work of nonfiction. Most names and incidents are used with permission granted to the author, others have been changed and characteristics related to them have been changed.

Printed in the United States of America on post-consumer recycled paper.

PREFACE

I want this book to be an inspiration to those who read it. I don't ever want you, the reader, to feel sorry for me. I am who I am today because of the experiences I have had in this lifetime. Each of us will have trials and trying times in our lives. Without these challenges we would be unable to grow and evolve.

I will share with you my experiences both physically and mentally and also my spiritual beliefs. I believe that each of us has an individual faith, not one of us fits into another's mold. Your relationship with your creator, the Supreme Being, God, the Universal Mind . . . whatever you "name" it--that relationship is personal and very private. I will share my Supreme Being relationship with you so that you may be able to allow yourself to tailor your own relationship and come closer and more reliant on "him" in every moment of every day that you live as a mortal human being. Open your heart and your mind, discover what YOU believe. Find organizations or faith leaders that can help you grow. Become more confident with yourself--be YOU, not someone that "they" want you to be. Believe in that little voice within you that you hear say, "I am here for you. Trust in me." God does speak to us.

CONTENTS

CHAPTER ONE

The winter weather had been nothing extraordinary. Standard spells of snow, frequent wind and colder temperatures. Ray, our twenty-one year old son, could not ride his motorcycle to and from work during those months from December to March, so he decided he would tear the bike down and do the modifications he couldn't stand to do without. One of the changes was designing and fabricating a new seat. As always, he had carefully studied and researched everything so he could create it completely on his own with the exception of sewing the vinyl seat cover. He created the mold and then the actual seat from fiberglass. He really wanted a leather cover, but firmly stood by his commitment not to consume or use animal products in any aspect of his life.

Almost everything was finished. He was ready to take the fabric to an upholstery shop. All he needed was the last shipment of parts.

The garage was a mess. Parts of the motorcycle were everywhere, along with all the tools that had landed where they were last used. Not only was he tearing apart his bike, he had also been working on the Triumph TR6 that his dad had passed on to him. So there were bits and pieces of the Kawasaki, but also nuts, bolts, engine pieces and parts, doorknobs, dashboard components--you name it--scattered everywhere. Some of it was neatly placed in boxes, but not much. How he knew where everything was I will never know, but I was frequently reminded not to move anything.

He set his sights and goals high, but his father, Rich, and I knew he was totally capable of outstanding results. So we patiently worked around his mess. He kept himself busy and it was wonderful seeing him operate in the adult world.

A couple of months earlier, in November, two days before Election Day, our German shepherd of twelve years died. It wasn't a sudden death, as he had suffered for many weeks with paralyzed hindquarters that led to a reduced appetite and failing health. He had been such a wonderful family member. It was so hard to let him go, but the day came that he gave us "the look" telling us he was done with this life. I called the vet and he came to give him the shot to let him sleep in peace forever. Ray and I lay on the floor with him until he breathed his last breath. Then we began to cry.

I had a meeting to conduct that evening so I gathered my wits and went, while Ray dug the hole and buried his companion. When I returned, I noticed Ray had cut his hair. When I asked him about it, all he could say was "It was for Alf." He had cut his long hair with his favorite knife, sprinkled the dog's favorite blanket with the hair and wrapped him up for good. Ray and I cried again. Not many words were spoken; we had developed a silent way of communicating. We both knew what the other was conveying. The pain was deep and there were no words.

On January 28 Rich had surgery to have a hip replaced after many, many years of pain. For many years we tried to convince him to see a doctor as he wouldn't and couldn't enjoy golf, hikes or camping. Even driving any distance beyond two hours was very uncomfortable for him, so there were no real family vacations after our trip to San Diego three years earlier. The surgery went well, adding one and a half inches to the length of his leg. He followed the doctor's instructions and the rehab was progressing nicely. The stairs were still a challenge for him, but he was improving by the day.

Before Christmas Ray came down with the flu followed by serious bronchitis. He was still fighting the bug. He went through two full rounds of antibiotics and missed three weeks of work in two months.

He hadn't been this sick since he was six years old. By about the second week in February he was finally himself again. He spent almost all of his time working in the garage on projects, or ordering parts over the Internet when he wasn't enjoying time with his friends. He had missed many holiday LAN parties (his network of computer friends) so now it was time to catch up.

The weather continued to improve and by the end of February we were enjoying a few spring-like days. The fruit trees needed trimming and we raked up the clutter that blew in over the winter, spending the weekend outside as much as possible.

Ray and I always enjoyed being in nature together. It was a good time for us to talk about everything under the sun. This weekend's conversation was filled to the brim with all the plans he had. He was scheduled to call the owner of some property he was considering buying in a nearby community. He could barely contain his excitement about the final shipment of motorcycle parts arriving on Monday. Finally he'd be able to put the bike together. He could ride it by the end of the week if everything came in and went together as planned. He was so happy to feel healthy again and have so many positive things happening.

Sunday evening came before we knew it. Rich and I began our mental preparation for work while Ray could barely wait for the next day to arrive. Around 10:00 we called it a night. Ray was in his room at his computer. He never enjoyed watching television, unless a program had to do with physics or how things work. I peeked my head in to say goodnight. Barely turning his head away from the computer screen, he replied "Good night. I can't WAIT for tomorrow!!! My parts will be here!" I said something indicating an appreciation for his coming day and reminded him to get to bed soon because his excitement would interrupt his sleep. He still needed to get as much rest as possible after all those weeks of being sick.

Just as I was feeling the euphoria of sleep, I heard what sounded like my turkey roasting pan hitting the kitchen counter and then the floor. I did notice that Ray had gone down the stairs to the kitchen a minute or two earlier and wondered what on earth he was going to try to cook up at this time of night. Rich and I sprung awake and asked each other, "What the hell was that?" Because Rich's mobility was still very restricted, I got up to see.

I walked the landing/hallway from our bedroom to his. "Ray?" No answer. I opened the door to his room which had been left ajar . . . no, not in there. Where was he? I didn't hear him cussing. And I didn't hear him go outside. Certainly he was aware of the racket. The noise came from the kitchen and I could see some of the kitchen from the landing. Certainly he would answer me if he were there. "Ray?" Still no answer. As I made it to the bottom of the stairs and came around the lazy-s curve into the kitchen I couldn't see him-- until I looked down. There were his feet sticking out from the end of the counter. He was on the floor . . . and he wasn't moving. Oh my God!!

As I took the remaining three extra steps I could see clearly. My son, the love of my life, was lifeless on the floor with a tiny trickle of blood coming from his right temple. He lay as if he was sleeping, snuggled up against the cupboards while under his head a small pillow of blood was forming. A handgun was on the floor a few feet away in front of the microwave and two pieces of a roundish dark wood were on the floor nearer the range. All I could do was to let out a blood-curdling scream with the word "NO!!!" mixed in somehow. Every bit of me was in the scream, my heart, my soul and my lungs-- my life.

With his cane, Rich was at the landing and down the stairs in an instant. I couldn't say anything. All I could see was Rich's skin going pale and the look of total despair, pain and disbelief. All he could say was "No! Ray… No!!" Rich was in the kitchen before I knew it and immediately got down on his good knee.

"Don't touch *anything*!" I said.

"I won't!!!" He snapped back at me.

Rich just kept saying, "Come on Ray . . . stay with us . . . stay here." I grabbed the phone and dialed 911. The call didn't go through the first time so I quickly dialed again. They answered the phone on the first ring. I yelled out our address and that my son had just shot himself in the head. I couldn't believe what I was saying--but it was the truth! Then I asked for emergency workers, ambulance . . . anybody! Everybody!!! NOW!!!! The operator started asking questions. "Is he alive?" I checked his pulse. "Yes! A pulse! HURRY!! Hurry!! We need someone NOW!!!" She said, "They are on their way." "Hurry! Hurry! Oh My God!!"

The rest of this ordeal is related in present tense to experience what it felt like moment-to- moment.

I grab the keys to the pickup so I can make room for the ambulance and EMTs while still on the phone with 911. "I don't hear sirens or see lights! Where are they?" I move the truck. Still no sirens or lights.

"Where are they!??!" I plead with them to call my boss and give them his cell number. He only lives a mile away! "HURRY!!" She puts me on hold, then comes back on the line, "Jeff is on his way." By this time I have been up and down the stairs about five or six times. I'm beginning to shake. The adrenaline is running hard throughout my body. Rich had been yelling "Are they here yet?" If I was in the house I went out to check, if I was outside I came back in only to tell my husband "No, Not yet." Then in the phone I would say, "HURRY!! HURRY!! Oh my God, his hands are turning blue! HURRY!!!" I could see the pillow of blood getting bigger. Every second seemed like forever.

5

I went outside again. Finally the first cop shows up. "HURRY!! Don't block the driveway for the ambulance!! Move your car!!" The EMTs are right behind him. There's my boss with his girlfriend . . . all I want is for someone to save Ray. Quickly we move into the house. We told them we didn't touch a thing and immediately moved away from Ray so they could save him.

Then . . . the quiet assessment . . . whispers . . . I know what that means. Rich tells me he's gone. "NO!!! NO!!!" I start shaking violently and I can't stop. My mouth goes dry. My boss's girlfriend holds me, Rich holds me. Rich can hardly stand, and we know to stay out of the way, so we sit in the formal living room on the other side of the partial wall that divides the kitchen from the formal dining and living areas.

More cops arrive. They ask who to call to pick him up and take him away. What is happening? This can't be real! I give them the name of the funeral home. David, the funeral director, was the only person I wanted to help me through what was coming.

I could hear everything! The opening of emergency medical kits, Velcro from this or that, plastic tearing, gloves snapping, every step each person takes, the sound of the fabric rubbing from their uniforms. I can even hear their breathing. I could have easily heard a pin drop with all the commotion.

The Chaplain introduces herself. I ask her to pray over him. Into the kitchen she walks, then comes right back. I can't believe what we are going through! Someone—don't have a clue who--asks if there is anything they can do. Rich says, "Turn back the clock!!"

Yes, turn back time! All we need is twenty minutes! That's all! I have no idea what the chaplain says, other than we need to drink fluids and eat anything our systems will allow. I ask her if she will please baptize Ray. She says she cannot. I don't remember if she gives me a reason.

Now I'm shaking so badly, feeling nauseated, and having trouble breathing. I have to poop, I have to pee, I have to throw up. My mouth is getting dry. And it just gets worse. I go outside and get some fresh cool air and get chilled, so I go back into the house. Then to the bathroom, then outside, then I sit for a minute or two on the sofa. I just can't sit still. My body is evacuating everything.

Somewhere in all the activity I ask that Rich, Jeff and his girlfriend hold hands and join me in prayer. I lead the prayer. I don't recall what I said except give us the strength we need to deal with what we are facing.

It was reality for us, right in our kitchen. Our son is gone. How could this happen? What the hell was he doing with a loaded firearm? Rich and I both told the detective to check Ray's computer to see what the hell he was watching. What kind of demented crap would make him do such a thing? We stressed early on that this HAD to have been an accident. Ray was too excited about tomorrow morning to do this on purpose. Just in case we were wrong, we demanded to see a computer scan. The detective reported Ray was watching a movie and viewing tattoos. There were no other sites he had visited that would raise alarm.

I request that any organs be harvested, as it was Ray's wish to be a donor. One of the team told me that would not be possible. So, no baptism and no harvesting. Why? Why were all my requests being denied? WHY?!

We are asked to move to another area of the house so the paramedics, law enforcement officers and the coroner can do their work. They suggest that we find a place where we will not be able to hear everything, as some of what they would discuss may not be pleasant.

Do we want to stay in our home or go to a friend's or to a motel? My boss Jeff encourages a motel room, and makes the arrangements. He returns and we sit in our respective seats in the family room. There we are. Just staring . . . there isn't anything to say. We both feel sick and numb. We can still hear most of what was going on upstairs. The Chaplain brings us a glass of water and soda crackers before she leaves.

Then we change our minds and make the decision to stay home and face what is going on. I will never forget hearing the whispers and the sound of the body bag being unzipped, rustled, then zipped again. Then the deep, heaving breaths of the men who had the awful task of taking him out of the house for the last time, their words ringing painfully in my ears.

"Got em?"

"Yeah."

"Wait . . ."

"OK."

Again, sounds of the body bag rustling; footsteps shuffling across the floor, out the door and down the outside steps.

I knew the mortician from town. His presence that night was a great comfort. He said he would take good care of Ray. The words he spoke along with his body language conveyed the depth of his caring. He made arrangements for someone to come in and clean the kitchen. They actually showed up during the night or very early the next day. Time didn't mean anything—we had lost the entire concept of time. Again I could hear all the rustling about, but now I was just numb.

I tell my boss I won't be coming into work tomorrow as he is leaving. It's a strange thing to say, but I say it.

Rich and I stay seated all night long, staring into the darkness of the room. With his post-surgery pain and physical restrictions, we cannot sit together or physically comfort one another unless I rise to lean over and hug him. All we can feel is pain in our chests and stomachs. As the sun rises and the darkness begins to fade into morning, a new day begins. This new day means nothing to us, only pain and loneliness.

The thought that refuses to leave me is the talk that Ray and I had no more than a week before the accident. It was one of those talks about religion that we had so often. He said, "There is definitely a Supreme Being or Supreme Power, but there is no devil or hell. And why are people afraid of dying? I'm not afraid to die! It's no big deal." He didn't say these things to impress or shock me; he truly believed what he said. His words were my only consolation during those first painful weeks.

CHAPTER TWO

Losing Ray has been absolutely the most difficult thing for me to deal with in my life. Many of us in this world lose people who are near and dear to us, but nothing can even come close to the loss of a child. There are no words that can express the depth or intensity of the physical and emotional pain a parent suffers.

Even though Ray was not the first child I had lost to death, it was the loss that ripped and tore my heart and soul to shreds.

It seems that my life has been a series of challenges. My physical stature had always been petite . . . I mean tiny. Everyone was so much larger than I was–unless of course they were a minimum of three years younger. Then and only then might I have a chance at being equal to or "superior." I lived my life with a serious inferiority complex. I saw myself as inferior, not only in a physical sense, but mentally as well. I was not particularly smart academically, I had little if any self-esteem and I found it in my best interest to keep my mouth closed and my opinions to myself. Should I ever be called on to defend my position, I just *knew* I didn't have a chance against people larger, stronger or more knowledgeable. I existed in my life . . . small and quiet.

I liken a person's life to soup: it takes many ingredients and a nice long time of simmering to blend all the flavors into a delicate, delicious food that is soothing to one's soul. The aroma of the soup can be smelled by others nearby yet they have no idea what it took to make such a smell so pleasing, nor do they know the true flavor. Such is the case with my life.

CHAPTER THREE

I came into this world in 1958, fifteen months after my brother Stephen. We lived in a pleasant home in a quiet neighborhood in Minnetonka, Minnesota. All the houses were generally the same size with small front lawns and fairly large backyards. Driveways and garages separated one house from the next. The earth under our white house sloped down on the right side so the garage was actually under the house on that side, unlike the light blue and soft yellow dwellings on either side of us where everything was on one level. Our front lawn had three concrete steps that led down to the driveway and the garage where my dad parked our old black Chevy sedan with its wide running boards. I had to stand on those ribbed running boards and stretch real tall to reach the door handle. Each of the concrete steps on the lawn came up to my mid-section. Climbing those stairs was a bit more challenging than the ones at the front stoop that only came up to my thigh. If I raised my foot up nice and high, I could get up those stoop stairs without using my hands, climbing on all fours.

The car was never parked in the small garage under the house because there were too many other things stuffed in there. In addition to the garage, the lower level of the house contained the laundry room with a big deep sink and large counter. This area was used for canning pickles, the fresh sharp smell of dill wafting through the air when my mother and aunt took on the task.

From there we could walk out into the backyard where mom had a small garden of tomato, cucumber and pepper plants. The tomato plants were so tall that they created a small forest for me and the peppers sported such a brilliant red as they matured.

My mom was born with one normal eye and one empty eye socket. She spent her entire childhood suffering through countless surgeries to make her face look something like normal. Gradually the surgeon was able to create an eyelid with grafted skin from other parts of her body, and, finally, the interior part of the socket was reconstructed well enough to hold a glass eye in place. The glass eye was shaped like a miniature bowl with uneven edges that had the iris and pupil painted on the bottom, matching her other eye.

Mom came from a well-to-do family. She and her older sister never wanted for any material possessions. Unlike her sister, who had countless friends and a very active social life in and out of school, mom spent her days in fear of being called a freak or worse—having her head beaten against the school's cinderblock wall by bullies. Her cocker spaniel would follow her to school in the morning and stand guard all day to be there for her if she needed a protective presence. Mother was not required to go home after school, the only house rule she needed to follow was to "Be home for dinner!" She always dreamed and prayed to look normal and to be treated with civility by society.

Her parents gladly took pictures of her sister, but every photo of mother was a posed side angle. There was never a photo of her full face, no happy activity shots. No memories of fun times were ever caught on film for her. She was an outcast in her own family. Loved, but treated differently.

Dad grew up the eldest son of five children. His father abandoned the family when Dad was very young. His mother did the best she could. He and his siblings could only wear shoes during the school year. He and his older sister did any odd jobs they could to help their mother make ends meet. By the time he was in eighth grade he had to quit school to work fulltime. He was a mason and contractor's apprentice when he met mom.

These two social misfits fell in love and married in 1956 when Dad was twenty-five and mom was twenty. My older brother Stephen was born one year later shortly after they purchased their first house.

My mother was a stay-at-home mom except when she took a temporary part-time position at the Animal Fair factory where they made stuffed animals that were sold worldwide. She would bring home lots of scrap material and it was fun to go through the bags trying to figure out which fur went to create which animal toy.

We had the privilege to be special animals for Halloween. I got to be a turtle. My mother used scrap fabric from work and a small bushel basket. I was so proud – I knew I looked just like a turtle. I remember how she painstakingly duplicated the striping of the turtle's tummy, painting it on the fabric. Then she took us out to trick or treat. The only place I recall trick or treating was a small soda fountain/dime store. I remember thinking I had the best costume ever!

She loved having fun with us when she wasn't working. In the winter she would make snowmen and other creatures. One winter she built a snow horse and took pictures of us with some neighbor kids "riding" it. In the summer she would enter Stephen and I in the local parades, dressing us up as Tarzan and Jane, complete with dirty charcoaled faces and skin, loin cloth and jungle attire from scraps of fur she got from work. Tarzan Stephen would pull me down the parade route in our red wagon that had magically been transformed into a cage.

Then there were those special moments of magic. The smell of my Aunt making pickles in the basement, the beautiful red maple leaves all over the ground, the smell of the tomato plant when you touched it, the vividness of the red contrasting with the green leaves of the garden plants. And then there was the little picture "machine." We would take a "picture" lay the "negative" on the sidewalk in the hot sun and watch the picture develop. I have never figured out just what that was, perhaps it was a wondrous Cracker Jacks box prize.

There were only a couple other kids in our little neighborhood to play with. There was a girl in the yellow house and a boy about Stephen's age that lived in the blue house. The boy was always mean to us, twisting our arms behind our backs or giving us Indian burns after begging us to trust him, promising that he wasn't going to hurt us. He came to visit one nice summer day while we had our little turtles out on the front stoop. The sun was hot but the cement stoop was cool, so mom said the turtles would be fine for a little while. The neighbor boy had only been there a short time when he decided to stomp on our turtles, smashing the poor little things all over the cement. Then he laughed. My brother and I were horrified. That neighbor boy was so good at inflicting injury. I could never understand why a person would ever want to hurt someone else. He got a sick satisfaction from inflicting physical and emotional pain.

Shortly before we left Minnesota Dad began work at the Tonka Toy factory. Stephen scored several brand-new Tonka trucks and machines. Dad obviously liked working there because he was just as excited as we were when he took us on a tour to see how the toys were made, explaining how everything worked. The twinkle in his eyes added to the magic of how toy trucks and tractors were made. It was fascinating to watch them move on the conveyor belt, getting sprayed or dipped in huge vats of paint.

On a fine November day in 1963 I found Stephen sitting Indian-style on the floor in front of the black-and-white television. It wasn't like him to sit mesmerized and motionless. Then I noticed the tears streaming down his face. "Why are you crying? Did you get in trouble? Did mom spank you?" I asked. He just shook his head. I saw what looked like a parade on the TV. "The President got killed," he said without even looking at me. I didn't understand who he was talking about but whoever it was sure made him sad. A few years later I learned that it was the assassination of JFK and it wasn't a parade at all; it was the funeral procession.

CHAPTER FOUR

In February of 1964 my father left us for a job in western Montana. The Tonka Toy factory didn't pay enough and he had been having trouble finding other work in Minnesota, so he took a cousin's offer to work at a sawmill in a remote town where there were enough trees for hundreds of years of work. He wasn't even there a month when he decided that he liked what he was doing. The tiny town tucked in the forest with a population of less than five hundred would be a fine place to raise his family.

In March, mom, Stephen and I moved from Minnesota to Montana on the railroad train. All of our belongings and our dog arrived later via moving van. Mother was about three months pregnant with my little brother and had to spend most of the trip in a sleeping compartment being attended to by a nurse. That left Stephen and me on our own so we would run down the aisles of the railcars. I would hesitate with deep-seated fear each time we would go from one car to the next because the gaps in the "floor" of the compartment that sealed one car to another seemed large enough to swallow me whole. The noises from the train rumbling down the tracks was deafening, the outside air blowing into the compartment and the combination of metal tracks, heavy wooden beams and earth whizzing by in a blur beneath my feet scared the wits out of me. One false step would mean the end of me, but there was no way I was going to let my brother have all the fun. It was such an adventure.

We left urban life in the land of a thousand lakes and landed in a place with creeks, mountains and millions of trees. No longer would we visit great aunts and uncles and Great Grandma "Pete" on the lakeshores. Our new hometown had a lake, but it wasn't anything like the lakes of Minnesota. In Minnesota the houses with their great lawns met the water. This lake had trees that grew to the water's edge. There were three public campgrounds with sandy beaches to enjoy. The rest of the shoreline was government or private property.

Our cousin's home was a basic, no-frills, small two-story home tucked in a thicket of trees in one of only two organized neighborhoods in the entire town. This little cluster of about thirty homes was referred to as "Dog Town," and a sign at the main highway listed each and every homeowner. Suddenly our cousin's home went from six to ten occupants.

Their children's bedrooms were at the top of a long narrow stairwell. Their youngest daughter was in high school and she had a lot of Snoopy and Charlie Brown toys in her room. Her room was neat and tidy and I was afraid to touch anything.

The sawmill was about a mile away, town proper about two miles. "Town" consisted of three bars, a post office, drug store, two small grocery stores with gas pumps, a laundry mat, one café and a tiny ice cream drive-up joint. If you looked down at your speedometer as you drove through, you could easily miss the entire town.

During our short stay with the cousins, my father had to go back to Minnesota because our house had been hit by a tornado. The twister had lifted our house off its foundation and thrown it against the neighbor's house, demolishing ours and damaging the other. I'm sure he went to take care of insurance business. Not much was said except how timely it was for us to have moved away when we did.

CHAPTER FIVE

We moved from the cousin's home into a tiny log cabin on a dude ranch within a few weeks. Not only had we moved to the wilderness, but now we were living in a lovely log cabin in the woods, just like in the movies with horses and cowboys. It was very small and only had three rooms – four counting the tiny little bathroom. Wildflowers bloomed amongst the trees around the cabin. There were tiny purple ones, pink ones and yellow ones: glacier lily, violets, shooting stars, wild roses, buttercups, mariposa lily, bear grass, Indian paintbrush, lupine, wild geraniums and fairy slippers. I had never seen so many beautiful things and they were everywhere!

We lived in the cabin for about four months–long enough for our dog to get pregnant and give birth to a litter of puppies under the front steps--and from where my mother went to the city more than fifty miles away. She went to see the doctor, as my little brother was attempting to arrive in this world a little too early. When she returned, she spent a lot of time in bed and Stephen and I had to start doing a lot of tasks that she had always done.

The owners of the dude ranch were very nice folks. They and their two children all dressed in true cowboy attire: jeans, western-style shirts and cowboy boots and hats. We had only seen cowboys on television. Stephen and I felt so special when they gave us a ride on a horse or in their stagecoach. This was an actual "wild west" cowboys-and-Indians stagecoach, just like you see in the old western movies. They mostly used it for the paying guests who came from the big cities in other states, but every once in awhile they would ask us if we wanted a ride.

The ranch house they lived in was a mansion compared to our tiny little cabin. Inside the front door was a huge reception / living room area. The ceiling went all the way up to the rafters–more than two stories high. To the left was the dining room, to the right was the stairway that led to all the guest bedrooms. The dining room was long and narrow with a table that seemed to go on forever, surrounded by so many chairs that I lost count. They would open their home for town hall dances and the entryway had no trouble accommodating the partygoers. The log cabin was also the place where a traveling salesman came and did yo-yo stunts and fascinating magic tricks for us.

If we were allowed to go beyond the ranch house to play, Stephen and I would head to the creek through the field where the horses grazed. I was so frightened crossing the field because when the curious horses would surround me, I could feel the hair on my legs move as their heavy legs came down next to mine, all but stepping on me with their massive hooves. I was sure they would trample me into nothingness there in the middle of the pasture. I felt so small compared to their huge, muscular bodies lumbering and towering over me, snorting their warm moist breath onto me to see if they could smell food.

The creek was a magical place with the soggy soil under my feet, bees, flies and butterflies buzzing, the sound of the rippling water as it gently rushed by, and the smell of green grass, fresh mint and pine trees in the moist air. I had never taken in so much nature–I felt I had been transported to another time, another world.

CHAPTER SIX

Sometime in late July we moved out of the cabin into the sawmill's cookhouse. This house was at least three times as big as the log cabin. It had a commercial flattop grill for cooking in the oversized kitchen. The dining room where the workers had eaten their meals was no longer used for this purpose, and the tables and chairs were nowhere to be found. This became our living room. My brother and I were introduced to cooking in that kitchen. After turning on the grill with the big dials, we each pulled a chair up to stand on; watching the egg splat onto the hot surface where it would do its bubble dance.

The bathroom consisted of a sink and shower. There was no inside toilet; an outhouse was a short distance from the back door. When it was storming or the coyotes sounded too close, I would be too frightened to go outside to the outhouse so I would tinkle in the shower, hoping that my mother wouldn't find out. Stephen was allowed to urinate in a can during the night–why couldn't I avoid the dark walk? Our bedrooms were upstairs. After living in the tiny log cabin it was scary to be so far away from our parents who slept downstairs. But it was a good place to live.

A long-time mill worker who lived in one of the tiny shacks next to the cook house, Hector, would come over to take showers, just as he had for many years. He had a very serious speech problem and drooled quite a bit. He would "shlure" nearly every word he spoke. I grew very fond of him quickly. He gave me the nickname "carrot-top" because of my red hair. That was how he always addressed me…."Hi Thcarrot Thop!!" he would call out. Hector was a good man with an infectious smile and a twinkle in his eyes.

My father was able to walk to work. There was only one other residence, a singlewide trailer between our home and the lumberyard with its huge entry gate. The sharp smell of fresh-cut pine filled the air, ever-present. Some days the scent would be so strong that my nose would tingle and I could actually taste the pine.

My parents joined a small group of families to found the Missouri Synod Lutheran Church in our community. Our home became a place of worship because the living room was plenty large enough to accommodate several rows of folding chairs without having to rearrange the furniture.

Within a month of moving into the cookhouse, mom delivered my little brother--a month early. Dad was earning enough now that he was able to save money to make a good down payment on five acres of land on the side of a mountain on the edge of the highway. The property was five miles north of town, and what seemed like forever away from any neighbors. There were eight overnight motel cabins being set on foundations at the base of the mountain along the highway, and one home a short distance from the highway on the other side tucked in the trees. One or two more homes existed further down that road, but they couldn't be seen from the highway. Everyone that I knew lived in Dog Town. The few people who lived north of town were strangers to me.

Dad got right to the business of creating a building site. There was no existing road or short route to our new piece of land. A well-worn road ran parallel to the highway at the bottom of the mountain below our land, so my father got permission to use a portion of it. It was a quarter of a mile from the highway to the mountain where Dad used the bulldozer to level a small spot on the mountainside for our house to sit. The entire road was barely wide enough for the family vehicle on a sheer mountain face. The only flat surface was the road itself.

From the flattened building site I could see for miles. Below, on the other side of the highway, were the meadows with a thick strip of trees that grew along the rivers banks, interrupting the expanse of grasses that lined the entire valley floor. On the other side of the valley rose the neighboring mountain range. Behind me was nothing but mountain wilderness reaching up to the sky. To the left and right the terrain gained altitude, creating a bowl of beauty.

The difficult task of constructing a home to call our own commenced, and by late October we moved into the shell with our beds. Strategically placed large cement squares set into the freshly disturbed soil served as the foundation. The house itself consisted of wooden stud framing wrapped in plastic with plywood flooring and a wood stove sitting smack-dab in the middle of the structure. That wood-burning device was our only source of heat. There was a brand-new outhouse several yards behind the house. Most of our belongings stayed at the cookhouse until there would be a place for them.

The weather was still warm but with each day that passed the nights got colder and colder. Within days we all helped get the insulation between the studs. Stephen and I would stuff the itchy pink material with its shiny paper liner in between the boards with mom right behind using the staple gun to secure the silver paper to the studs. While we did that, Dad applied a layer of plywood siding on the exterior. We had electricity, but nothing like what you might imagine. A couple of wires with either a light bulb hanging down or an outlet receptacle at the end were strung across the ceiling and floor. Interior studs created the framework of what would become separate rooms, so for now the light from that single bulb traveled far. There was no running water. At about the same time that we insulated, Dad upgraded the electricity and we got a used oven/range installed in what would become the kitchen. He also found a used one-piece kitchen sink cabinet and a makeshift counter top that someone else had thrown out.

Water could be collected at the relative's or at one of the two small grocery stores in town. The vessels that held the precious liquid were two metal milk cans. We used as little water as possible and re-used as much as we could. There were two plastic tubs to wash and rinse dishes. Baths were completely out of the question the first few years. Sponge bathing was how we got clean; using a washcloth moistened and rinsed in a bowl containing a few cups of water heated on the range. After making it through the first winter, Dad created a slue system under the house so we could dump used water down the sink. The wooden trough took the water to the other side of the house where it would spill down an embankment.

The winter months made transporting water a huge chore, so we would use as much melted snow as possible for everything except drinking. As the snow collected on the road between the highway and the house, the road gradually became impassable. If the snow wasn't too deep, the car could almost make it to the top of the driveway and we would only have to walk a couple hundred yards, but later in the winter we had to walk the entire distance. The cans of water and groceries were pulled up the road on a sled. It was never easy trudging through the snow pulling a load uphill, so we would all take turns carrying the baby or pulling the sled.

Running water finally came to my family when I was a sophomore in high school. It's hard for me to imagine my father hauling those heavy cans for 10 years.

Major shopping trips to the city 60 miles away were done approximately once a month. The grocery stores in the little hometown carried a limited inventory of goods. All building supplies, with the exception of wood planks, came from the city. The drive to the city took over an hour in good weather and up to two and a half hours in winter.

The construction of our home happened very, very slowly. Things were added as my parents could afford them. Plastic windows and insulation walls remained for many, many years. I remember how happy I was when we got our first glass window. What a celebration that was!

When Dad finally got a used tub in what would someday be our bathroom, we were allowed to take a bath–but only once or twice a year. It took more than one full milk can of water, so on that rare occasion we were allowed a very short amount of time to clean and frolic. All members of the family shared the same tub of stove-heated water that was never more than 2 inches deep. Talk about a treat!

My petite stature prohibited me from participating in the physical demands of construction work, so it was my job to provide all care for my little brother while my mom, Dad and Stephen worked the hammers, picks, shovels and other tools. I was six and my little brother was only two months old when we moved into the shell of a home. Mom had already taught me the basics of cooking and cleaning while on pregnancy bed-rest. All tasks took extra effort for me--to cook or wash the dishes I had to stand on a chair to reach and use the sink or stove. Changing diapers and other infant care was easy in comparison.

In addition to being in charge of my baby brother, I was also required to do the family laundry. Once a week I would be dropped off at the laundry mat. Mom usually helped me get the washers loaded – then she'd leave. She would return in time to help fold the last of the clothes and carry the heavy baskets to the car. In order to load and unload the clothes from the washer or dryer, I would have to climb into one of the carts, insert the coins and detergent, and then repeat the climb to retrieve the clothes. Then I would push the cart full of wet clothes to the dryers, throw as many in the dryer as I could reach, get back in, empty the cart of the rest and deposit the coins in the dryer. The laundry mat prohibited riding in the carts, but it was the only possible way for me to get the job done. Sometimes Stephen would be required to help me. I always liked it when he would help.

We would give each other rides in the carts while waiting for the washers and dryers to complete their cycles.

During the first few years there was a miniature golf course behind the laundry mat. I never went outside unless Stephen was with me, so when he had to help we would watch people play on the bright green fake grass. I liked the windmill and other colorful obstacles--I thought it was such a fascinating place. The harsh winters took their toll on the fake grass and wooden fixtures, so they didn't last long.

After moving from the cookhouse, church services were held in the home the Pastor was renting. By spring the church had acquired property adjacent to the Pastor's home. Plans were drawn and construction began on an A-framed church building. There wasn't any money to pay contractors, so everyone in the congregation, young and old, worked together to build the house of worship. I passed nails to those with hammers, retrieved small tools or glasses of water and helped gather the scraps of wood and bent nails strewn about when I wasn't caring for babies and toddlers. Within weeks the beautiful church was completed. Everyone claimed ownership and we all beamed with pride.

CHAPTER SEVEN

Summer in Montana was the time to explore our vast, wild surroundings. Because she grew up in the Land of a Thousand Lakes, mother loved the water, so discovering the best swimming holes was top priority. There was a small body of water in Dog Town named The Pot Hole. Everyone in Dog Town went to swim there. I spent more time lying on the dock watching the crawdads on the pond floor than actually swimming. We also tried out the campground beaches of the big lake. There were no docks at the campgrounds but there was a lot more sandy soil.

Each summer Stephen and I were enrolled in swimming lessons. There was no swimming pool in town, so lessons were always held at the lake on a tiny beach away from one of the campgrounds.

When I was seven, after a fun day of swimming, I was thrown from the moving car onto the gravel road when we took the ninety-degree turn off the highway onto Dog Town Road. All I had on was my swimsuit. We were in a station wagon and the back seats were down to make a flat passenger compartment for us kids. I was leaning on the door right behind the driver. As the car made the turn onto the gravel road, the door flung open and centrifugal force hurled me out. Our day of fun was over in an instant. My mother rushed me to the nurse who lived in town. I had no broken bones, just a backside embedded with gravel. Bits of rock had to be picked out of my back. I never leaned on another car door until I was an adult, knowing for sure that the door was completely latched.

Summer was also the time to harvest food. Mom learned quickly what the wilds had to offer. She would take us into the woods to pick huckleberries, serviceberries, elderberries and wild raspberries for pies, jams and jellies. Wild strawberries grew everywhere but there were never enough in one spot to make anything with. Those just made wonderful taste treats.

With no school in session, my social interaction was limited to church, babysitting jobs, swimming lessons and vacation bible school, so I always looked forward to them. I was shy and quiet so I didn't "interact" a lot. Just being part of the crowd fulfilled my needs.

Living in such a remote area sharpened my sense of smell and seemed to give me the ability to hear things from very far away. I could hear the school bus coming from more than two miles away. How does that work? This wasn't flat land, this was a mountainous area with all kinds of wildlife and trees and dips, curves and peaks in the roadway. When the breeze would blow I heard the trees talking to one another—the big Ponderosa Pines and slender Lodgepole Pines gently moving from side to side. A gentle group sigh could be heard in addition to their branches making small creaking and popping noises from the stretching movements created by the wind, just as if they were waking up from sleep. Their noises would be answered by the Quaking Aspens gently rattling their leaves and creating smaller creaking, snapping sounds.

I could hear the night birds and owls way down at the river and the coyotes howling every night in the wilderness up behind the house and all the way across the valley below. It always sounded as if they were in our backyard. Sometimes they were, but they were usually quite a distance up the mountain. It was fascinating to listen to the nearest pack and then hear the replies of the other packs on the other side of the valley. A couple of times I quietly crept up the mountain to watch the animals in action. Nature was always saying something and I loved listening.

CHAPTER EIGHT

After spending the first winter in the framed house, struggling to keep warm, mom and Dad accepted an offer from the owners of the eight-unit motel along the highway to run the place for several months. The motel had an office building where they had a washer and dryer, kept all the supplies, and sold pop, candy and small cans and boxes of easy-to-fix foods. There was an ice machine behind the office so when it was real hot or when Stephen and I got thirsty we would take handfuls of ice out of the bin where the cubes collected. The pop machine was a big metal chest. You had to lift the lid, put in your money and pull out the glass soda bottle of your choice. Every once in awhile, mom would let us have a grape or orange soda if we had done all our chores without complaining.

Dad would be able to work on the house after a full day of work at the mill without the rest of us in his way. If he needed to leave the place open to the weather, he could.

Taking on the motel management gave us a place to live—even though it was only a one-bedroom cabin with the bare essentials for a kitchen. It was warmer than our house up the hill and we had running water so we could take showers and go to the bathroom inside. Stephen and I didn't mind sleeping in the living room with our baby brother. Even though I was still in charge of the baby and housekeeping, I had to help clean and prepare the cabins for new guests. My primary task was to strip the beds and put clean linens on them nice and tight like in the military. My older brother was kept busy with his own set of chores.

I would work at that motel off and on until I left town after graduating from high school. The owners would hire me to scrape paint, help prepare the rooms for guests or watch the guest's children. When I was older they had me "manage" the place for a whopping seventy-five cents an hour.

Stephen and I would play in the woods between the house and motel, scaling the steep embankment that was formed when they flattened the area for the cabins, pretending to be cowboys and Indians, building new roads with his Tonka Toy trucks or simply trying to ride those wonderful lodge pole pine trees. If they were thin enough to bend down and straddle, we could bounce up and down and take a tree ride.

Our German shepherd/golden retriever mix dog named Princess was our constant companion. She was such a good dog and we were so glad that Mom and Dad went to the trouble of letting her make the trip from Minnesota with us. Princess would greet all the motel guests as if they were long-lost friends. One day she growled and threatened to bite a man who was traveling alone. My folks had to tie her up because she was so aggressive. A week or so after he vacated, we found out he was wanted for murder and Princess was released from her tether. She had proved without a doubt that she could tell if a human had good or bad intentions.

We lived in the motel for that entire winter. As Thanksgiving approached, the number of guests dropped off to almost nothing as soon as hunting season ended and there wasn't enough snow for snowmobiling. Mom had more time to cook so she decided to make an apple pie from fruit she preserved the year before. The pie was a real treat. Somehow her pies tasted better than the ones I made. I had my slice about half gone when suddenly I experienced incredible pain in my throat. I grabbed my neck as if I was strangling myself, but the pain increased. I was sure I was dying. The searing pain made it impossible to speak. I could only scream.

"Oh my God!! What's wrong??!!" my mother repeatedly yelled at me. I couldn't answer.

Both of my brothers began crying because of my hysteria. Blood came out of my mouth and I could see from the look on Mom's face. She knew it wasn't good. She looked sad, confused and helpless. She leaped the few steps to the kitchen and grabbed something from the sink. The apples had been canned in glass jars. She lifted a jar from the sink. Quickly she ran her forefinger around the top edge, suddenly stopping when she felt the tiny dip. "It's glass! She's swallowed a piece of glass!!"

Dad grabbed a small piece of bread and firmly demanded I eat it. Never seeing him this adamant, I fearfully forced myself to chew. "Swallow it!!" he ordered. I was scared to death to swallow anything…what if it made the pain worse? "Swallow!!" Somehow I managed to get it down my throat. Magically the pain dropped to a manageable level. "Better?" Dad asked. I still couldn't speak so I shook my head "yes." As I began to gather myself back together I noticed Mom was crying. With her face buried in her hands, she confessed that she had noticed the chip missing in the top edge of the jar, but made the pie anyway. She felt awful!

CHAPTER NINE

In the winter my older brother and I would build snow igloos. We used toboggans or inner tubes and saucers down the hills. We would put three or four pairs of socks on (wool ones on the outside) and hike up the mountain as far as we could. When we got as far up as we wanted to go, we would run as fast as our legs could carry us and slide back down to the house. Having multiple layers of socks acted as small snowshoes and we were able to glide on the top of the snow much of the time.

When the weather warmed that spring, my parents moved into our new house permanently.

My brothers and I slept in the upstairs attic area. House plans changed as construction continued, and, for a few years, we had a stairway. Then we had a ladder as the new plans did not accommodate a stairway. Extra belongings were stored upstairs where the packrats lived in the attic/eave area and where, as we got older, we separated our rooms by hanging sheets or blankets.

Once, before the stairs were removed, while the three of us were playing before bedtime, I accidentally kicked my little brother off the bed, sending him right through the plastic lining the studs down several feet to the stairs. Thank goodness he didn't get hurt.

I don't recall if it was the second Christmas in the house or a few years later, but my brother plugged in the tree lights, and suddenly the entire wall was on fire. I was hysterical. Never in my life had I lost it emotionally that way until I was forty-six.

The walk to the outhouse didn't seem quite as far as it did when we lived in the mill cookhouse. It was still challenging as the coyotes and other wild animals lived in the same forest we did. I remember my brother digging two holes in those twelve years. He was also charged with digging a well. As he would get another three or four feet dug, my father would add another cement casing. The well got to be twenty or so feet deep with no evidence of water before my parents finally let him stop digging. A four by eight sheet of plywood covered the hole for "safety." I don't know if that hole was ever filled in.

We had rabbits hutched halfway down the hill to the motel. The only advantage to that was a spring on that piece of property, so we could catch water for them there instead of hauling it. When I was fifteen, my father was finally able to install a pump and pipe the water up to the house. I don't have a clue how the goats got water, but we had to walk the horses to a nearby creek a half mile away.

I was taught early on to milk the goats. I didn't mind the task as I loved the goats, but having to feed, water and milk them before going to school was demanding. One morning we were running late and my brother and I hurried to tie the goats to trees for the day. Mom was home all day, but when we returned from school we discovered the oldest goat, the most gentle and friendly that gave the most milk, had choked to death. We had accidentally tied a slipknot that morning and mom had never checked on them.

When it came time to slaughter the young billy goat, my older brother thought he had gotten sufficient advice on how to get it done quickly and painlessly. He took a rifle and shot the goat right between the eyes. The goat cried and followed my brother around. He shot it again . . . no change. He struck it on the head thinking that some hard blows would knock him out. The only thing that happened was the rifle broke in two. He ran to the house and grabbed a sharp knife returning to slit the throat of the poor animal.

The animal just stayed real close, expecting my brother was going to help him. It was a sickening experience.

One day I was walking from the house to my father's shop, focusing on not spilling the milk in the bowl I was holding. I wanted to deliver every drop to the cats and kittens, so I couldn't look up. As I walked I was calling, "Here kitty, kitty, kitty!" There was a lot of racket. I looked up to discover that I was twelve inches away, nose to nose, with a black bear. I said one last "Kitty?" as I looked the bear in the face. We were both so frightened that he ran into the woods and I ran to the house.

CHAPTER TEN

Animals were always a part of our lives. After our first winter in the "new house," we acquired a couple more cats to help keep the mouse and packrat population down. In addition to rabbits and goats for meat and milk, we had chickens. Skunks got a lot of the chickens and someone else's dogs came from more than a mile away to kill our rabbits.

For some reason my parents thought they wanted to buy a pregnant horse that constantly coughed. No one in the family was serious about becoming an equestrian rider; Stephen would ride her every now and then and I would only get on her after a lot of convincing. My legs were so short, spreading out so straight, that it was very difficult for me to keep my center of gravity and there was absolutely no way for me to grab the sides of the animal with my heels. As the horse moved with each step, my bottom would ride to one side or the other until I would just slip off. We kept the colt until he was a year old and the mare until she was ready for the cannery. In the hottest part of summer, after the little spring runoff brooks dried up we had to walk the horses to a creek just over a half mile away for water.

One day law enforcement came to see us because someone had turned us in for animal cruelty; starving our horse to be exact. I honestly don't know if the animal was starving or not. All I knew was that she was sick because of her chronic cough. At that age I believed everything my parents told me.

We had so many cats, as my parents never neutered an animal. My mother preferred killing them or capturing them and hauling them the sixty miles to the animal shelter in the city. One day she was very upset with me and got me so angry that I picked up the kitten that I loved the most and I threw it. The kitten hit a cardboard box and broke its neck. It landed on the floor softly meowing with its head bobbing. I have never owned one of those bobble-head toys after killing my kitten. My dad had to take it out and thump it on the head to put it out of its misery.

I have always thought of animals as more than just creatures. Each one has a personality; some were easier to get to know, like the animals we choose to have as pets vs. the ones raised for food or those that remain wild. Of all the animals I was exposed to--horses, goats, chickens, rabbits, dogs and cats, turtles, guinea pigs and canaries--the dogs, cats and goats seemed more "human" to me. The horses, rabbits, guinea pigs and canaries also had personalities, but it took me longer to understand them and I never quite connected with the turtles. I cried every single time an animal died as if I had lost a member of my family. If it was killed for food I would gather my wits more quickly by convincing myself that God meant for certain animals to be sacrificed for our health. I could not grasp the purpose of each animal's life, but I always sensed that they were each here for a specific reason.

The love and tenderness that I received from animals was something that no human being had ever delivered to me. Unlike humans, I was never purposefully injured or hurt by an animal. The guinea pig nearly bit the end of my finger off because I was holding the piece of carrot–my finger was just in the way. The bear I walked into meant no harm–he was just hungry. The horse didn't buck me off--I just couldn't stay on, and the cat that clawed deep into my arm was simply frightened. Their souls were gentle, but they had skills that made them seem mean at times; those skills were meant to help them stay alive. I too am an animal, just more complex. And God made us all and loves us all.

When I was young I never understood how adults *knew* that animals never went to heaven. How would they know that? Now I believe that they do indeed go to heaven.

CHAPTER ELEVEN

Just as with cooking, I was also taught to sew at an early age and won a blue ribbon at the county fair for a dress that I had made in fourth grade. I was part of the 4-H Club and had to submit my dress and other projects. I did not do well on any other item or project, but I was so proud of that dress. That spurred me on to enjoy sewing from that day forward. I wasn't allowed to make many items, as fabric was too expensive, so I often used scraps or socks to make doll clothes. Classmates in elementary school asked if I could make their doll clothes. I said yes, but I never followed through.

With two years of every day infant/toddler care, I was also a very good little "mother," so Mom got me my first job—babysitting. The baby I was charged with was almost two years old and half as tall as I was, so carrying him around when he got hurt or was crying was quite a workout for me. I didn't mind the work because I loved children. I must have done a good job because as word got around town, I ended up having so many job offers I would frequently have to turn someone down. The only downside to the job was that I would always have to walk to and from the highway, no matter the time of year, no matter the weather. Our driveway offered no room for error, so none of my "employers" would attempt it.

I never really minded walking the quarter mile to the bus stop at the end of our driveway, that is until I joined the band in sixth grade and decided to play the baritone. I loved the sound of the instrument, low and strong, but that thing was as big as I was! I tried using our little red wagon as a cart but the road was too rough. The packed soil of the tire tracks wasn't quite wide enough for all four of the wagon tires and the ground between the tire tracks was too uneven with all the plants and rocks claiming the space. The wagon would repeatedly tip over so it didn't take too long for me to decide that I needed to learn a smaller instrument. I really wanted to play the flute but there was no room for another flute in the school band, so it was the clarinet for me. Our band was small—maybe twelve students. The elementary and high school each had a student body consisting of 100 or fewer students (K through 8 and freshman through senior).

Being so small for my age always seemed to create situations for me. When I was in eighth grade I qualified for a spelling bee competition in a neighboring community 30 miles to the north. A teacher for that school found me in the hallway and asked me where my mother was. I told her that I was in the spelling bee and what grade I was in. She told me I was lying and that I couldn't possibly be old enough to be in school yet. She grabbed my hand, dragging me through the school until she found my teacher. Then she let go and walked away, never making any apologies for being so harsh. I also remember my mother telling stories that she would have to make sure that any new bus drivers were introduced to me so they would allow me on the bus as I had been refused rides by substitute drivers.

Many high school students were bussed in from three nearby communities north, south and east of our small town. Some of them came from 50 miles away and had to be on the bus for no less than two and a half hours every morning and afternoon. All buses carried kindergarten through senior high school students. Our bus driver was so kind. He would allow students to bring music to play on his eight-track player and several times a year he would stop at the local store so the kids could get a snack for the ride home. He would surprise us all by buying a case of oranges or apples or he'd bag up some candy for every rider. He loved what he did and he took care of all of his "children." When I entered high school, I found out that he was also the study hall "teacher."

CHAPTER TWELVE

Living in a partially constructed home with no running water did nothing for our social status. My family was always looked down upon by community members—we belonged to the lowest class of citizens. The unspoken class system went something like this: there were those who simply had tons of money, those who had money because they owned their own business, those who made a decent living and had a nice home, those who didn't make much money but still lived in a decent home, those who didn't have much and didn't live in a very nice home, those who didn't have much at all and lived in a dilapidated home, those with little to no money and lived in a shack--and then there was us, those with little to nothing, living in a structure that should not be inhabited, and God forbid . . . no running water! I considered myself "normal" except that I didn't have the luxuries of a finished house and plumbing. I knew we didn't live like everyone else, but I never understood how that would have any bearing on how well one was liked or not liked.

Mom refused to acknowledge our social status, making sure that Stephen and I belonged to organized clubs like Cub Scouts, Brownies and 4-H.

When I would be included in a group transported by another parent, they would forget that I was in the car because I was always so quiet and intimidated by everyone. Frequently I would be taken to their home or taken a few extra miles from mine before they would realize that I was there. I never spoke up to ask them to stop. My entire body would freeze at the mere thought of speaking to an adult. I would always tell myself to say something, but my lips were locked and they were not going to move.

I never had more than one or two friends and never spent the night at someone else's home until I was in high school. The only visitors we ever had were relatives who came from Minnesota or the Pastor of our church who ate dinner with us twice.

I never had a birthday party of my own at home. Mom always said it was because no one would risk driving up the road to the house. I rarely played with friends at their homes either. The only birthday party I ever had was when my friend in second grade was having hers, and she invited me to have mine with her. We were exactly the same age and we were very, very close friends. She got eighty percent of the gifts—she and her family owned a lakeshore hotel and resort, so they were accepted members of society. The children and their parents were there for her, not me. Some of them were kind enough to bring an extra gift for me. I enjoyed being there. Celebrating her birthday was fun. We would never celebrate our birthdays together again. At the end of our third grade year her family moved back to Alaska.

Mom did her best, always making sure each of us kids had a cake and something special for our birthdays. I would often have to sit outside while she finished the cake and decorated it so it would be a surprise.

CHAPTER THIRTEEN

My mother was very intense and made us work very hard, but she could also be a lot of fun. She made sure that we saw every Walt Disney movie, she enjoyed all types of music and she even started water fights inside the house. As soon as I started high school, my mother had had it with living in an inadequate home in a community with little to no social opportunities. She decided she was going off to work and attend college in the city. Her thirst for knowledge and taste for culture was at the bursting point. She'd arrange for me to attend some of the symphony concerts or holiday choral concerts with her. The college and movie theatre were in the city, so these arrangements weren't easy tasks, given that the family usually only had two vehicles for four or five drivers.

She had been threatening to leave my father for years, and I had acted as counselor many times. I recall a "session" when I was ten. I will never forget that day when she told my father she was leaving. He went up to the attic. I pleaded with him to either tell her to stay or tell her to go. He was crying. I had never seen my father cry and don't recall seeing it again until I was 46. All he could tell me was that he loved her with all his heart and soul and he would never renege on his wedding vows. I didn't understand it. All I could see was how miserable she was and how she always blamed him for her misery. I was tired of her threats. And if she was so miserable, why was she staying?

My older brother and I were fine. We both worked. We knew how to cook, and I had been raising my little brother for years. What would change if she left?

She got a job and made arrangements to stay in the city during the week. She would only come home on weekends. Within a year or two she started college. She got student loans and grants for tuition and housing. She made it work. I was proud of her for her determination.

In about a year I had my driver's license. With Mom gone, I became the "mother" and was the one to make my father's lunch, set his alarm, get him up when it rang, make his breakfast and drive him to work if we needed the car for school. I made sure my younger brother got his homework done and got off to school. I even attended his parent teacher conferences. I don't know how we did it. My older brother was always there, and we were very close, but we sure fought a lot.

I was always jealous of Stephen. It started while we were in the mill cookhouse. When he became ill, he got special treatment and was encouraged to stay in bed. I had to help make him Jell-O water. When I was sick, I was required to iron, mend clothes, or do other chores. I was never left to rest when I was sick, I was never waited on, and never once was I offered Jell-O water. If I needed a glass of water, I had to get it myself. By the time I was in high school I knew never to stay home, no matter how sick I felt.

When it came to other house rules, my brother was always allowed to break them. However, if I ever mis-stepped, I would get the wooden spoon, belt and/or more chore assignments. I wonder now if that was my mother's way of reconciling the hard physical labor she put my brother through. I wasn't required to do the dirt moving, as my stature just wasn't able to accommodate that kind of work. My jealousy got worse after my brother had been picking on me and being so mean that I finally slugged him in the stomach. I caught him off-guard and he doubled over with pain and ran home crying to Mom. When he told her what happened, I got the belt and he was told to not be mean to me. Little did she know how many times he had hurt me over the years.

CHAPTER FOURTEEN

When I was a sophomore, the niece of a family in town came to live with us. Her parents, who lived in Seattle, were divorced and she had become too much for either parent to deal with, so they sent her to live with her aunt and uncle. It turned out she was a bit much for them as well. She and my brother were classmates and became fast friends. The first year of staying with us, she got involved with a group of girls in the school who were quite wild.

They robbed the medicine cabinets in their homes, put all the pills in a bowl and each consumed a handful. I remember how frightened she was that she was actually dying. The nearest hospital was an hour away. It was extremely scary for me too, as I didn't have a clue what to do for her except to stay by her side and tell her how crazy she was for even trying the pills. It scared her (and I) enough that she never did drugs again after that. She continued to live with us until after graduation, when she and my older brother, who had become romantically involved with her, moved to Tacoma where he was stationed in the Army. She had become my "sister" and we were very close.

My high school years were busy. I wasn't the best academic student, but I absolutely loved P.E., Home Economics, French, Chorus, Band, cross-country and track. I was not good at any organized sport. I babysat for many families until my senior year. I had gained quite a reputation and usually had childcare jobs to choose from. I never had much money, however--I only earned twenty-five cents per hour, if they paid me at all. I didn't have a very active social life until I got my driver's license. As part of trying to fit in and be accepted into any social circle, I took up cigarette smoking at fifteen. I was successful at keeping the knowledge from my parents until I moved out. I picked up beer bottles along the highway and redeemed a lot of coupons to cover the cost of fifty-cent packs of cigarettes.

The first time I flew was in a four-seat Cessna that my "sister's" father owned. He had come from Seattle to pick us up so we could spend a week with him during the summer. In such a small airplane you could feel every air pocket and the plane would instantly drop or float up depending on which way you entered the "pocket." I was a little nervous but knew I was riding with an experienced pilot. It was fun.

CHAPTER FIFTEEN

In my entire childhood, our family took only two vacations. At age ten, we went to Minnesota to see family and at age fifteen, we took a trip to Anaheim and Hemet, California – again to see family. Minnesota was uneventful, but the trip to California was a trip to remember.

There were six of us (family plus the teenaged "sister" who had just begun to live with us) all squished into a tiny Subaru sedan together with our luggage. The car had no air conditioning, travelling in the heat of the summer. I immediately developed a rash. My younger brother and I were the smallest, so he was sitting on me, wearing a mesh tank top. The mesh made it possible to scratch my itchy arms. It was the only bit of relief that I could find. A stop at a medical facility only provided some anti-itch ointment, but no diagnosis. We went to Disneyland and Universal Studios—both magical places. We saw Lucille Ball's dressing room and Alan Alda on the grounds at Universal. In Disneyland, I loved the night-time light parade and the mansion where I watched holographic figures of people dancing in the room below. The figures were dressed in colonial or earlier attire and I remember feeling like I had lived that life centuries ago and how privileged I was to get a glimpse of something I already knew. That was a very strange feeling. It was the first time I glimpsed a past life.

Something similar happened to me while I was in the Girl Scouts. The troop went on a trip to the state Capitol in Helena. I had never been there before. As we drove around near the Capitol building we passed a two-story house that was obviously one of the original homes built in the city. It was still being occupied as a residence. As soon as my eyes focused on the house I felt strange. My mind showed me the inside of the structure. I was a small child at the base of the stairs just inside the front door. I could see rooms to the left and right of the entryway. Straight ahead were the stairs with the banister on the left, a wall on the right. The wood was dark and I felt like I was chasing another child up the stairs. There was no mistaking that my mind was telling me this was my home.

It was confusing to me, but it was so real that I never forgot the feelings and the visions I experienced that day. I tried to talk to my mom about it but she dismissed it in such a way that I never confided in anyone else until I was an adult. After high school I returned to Helena to visit friends, passing by that house. Again, I had the same visions and sense of belonging there. I have never explored the history of that home. If it still stands, I know for certain that I would have the same "flashback." And whenever I listen to baroque music I always feel like I'm in a room with the original instruments being played for me. I don't just enjoy the music, I feel an attachment to it.

CHAPTER SIXTEEN

As a child, my parents determined what faith I would practice--Missouri Synod Lutheran Christianity. I took all the classes that the church had to offer, attended all summer vacation bible schools, went to the faith's church camp once, maybe twice, and attended every potluck, special service, choir practice and bible study meeting there was. My family was one of the core members of the church so we went to everything.

We had one pastor for several years, then he moved on. The vicars and other pastors who succeeded him never stayed very long. Things would always get ugly and the faith leader would leave. For many years I didn't understand what went wrong, but by the time I was in high school I could see that unnamed members of our congregation would make nasty claims and accusations against the pastors. I felt very much like we had a congregation full of Satan's helpers instead of faithful worshipers. I never understood why those members made it their mission to expel the leader of our church. What kind of Christian would do such a thing? Did all the messages that we heard each Sunday not mean anything to them?

I knew well our denomination's understanding of the scriptures, but that never answered my question: "Why can't our church participate in the annual community faith Sunday service?" All the other churches in our community participated except us. Why? Wasn't there the constant message: "Thou shalt love thy brother," and "We are all brothers and sisters in the eyes of the Lord." Why could we not enjoy one Sunday with our brothers and sisters of other denominations?

The answer always came across that the other faiths weren't good enough. You could only get to heaven if you were Missouri Synod Lutheran. What?!! Really? I silently questioned that.

I was raised to never question an adult, especially about religion. Children were meant to be seen, not heard. I don't feel that my parents were extreme about it, but I certainly never interrupted adults in conversation. I was easily intimidated by anyone who was larger or older than me. With my very tiny stature it meant that almost everyone made me feel inferior. I was always the smallest one in my class . . . I just felt that it was just my place in life to be an observer, not a participant. I acted like a mouse in the corner and any confrontation or sudden movement would make me want to hide. I am not quite sure how these attributes made me a good babysitter . . . but that was my gift. I was a good caregiver to little ones.

CHAPTER SEVENTEEN

In high school, our church had a visit from the Lutheran college students from Oregon. They presented their message of faith through music; vocal and instrumental. I clearly remember them stopping in the middle of a song… "Come on people! This is not a funeral! Let us see the joy in your hearts. Clap your hands…Praise the Lord!! It's okay to show how you feel." I don't recall many members loosening up. The only word that comes to mind is "stuffy."

I was in the balcony area where many of the young people had gathered. We felt we had a better view from there and the acoustics were clearer, too. About three quarters the way through the performance, I began to cry. The message I was hearing, the happy, free body language I was seeing filled my soul with joy. I was smiling from ear to ear from the center of my being. I could feel the spirit of the Lord within me. It felt so good that I couldn't help but cry. As soon as I began to let myself shed a tear, it was like the floodgates had just been breached. A lake of tears within me hurried to escape. I felt as though there was a beam of light coming directly from God to me through me . . . only me . . . no one around me could sense or feel it. It was very personal and very powerful. Those around me noticed the tears and asked if I was okay. I just replied with a smile "I'm fine." They never understood.

I never felt like that again.

In my senior year of high school, my mother's cousin, who had been the matriarch of the family we first lived with, was dying of muscular dystrophy. My mother and I made a trip to the city to see her and do some shopping. When we arrived at the hospital and entered her room, I was taken aback with what I saw. She appeared to be sleeping in the most peaceful state I had ever seen. There was a glow of peace that cannot be described unless you have witnessed it. In addition to other monitors, she was hooked up to a ventilator that was doing her breathing for her. The sound of the machine hissing periodically seemed so loud, breaking the peace in the room. Her husband and children were there with her. They had told us that just before we arrived she had opened her eyes, smiled, and stated that she was entering the pearly gates and the angels were there with her. Our visit was short; we said our goodbyes and headed home.

As soon as we got home, my father told us that they had called from the hospital about ten minutes after we had left her room to say she had died.

I was confused by what I had witnessed. She had only attended two or three church services in ten years, and I had been taught that if you didn't attend church there was no place for you in heaven. If she wasn't going to heaven, hell must be a pretty nice place! No one could be that peaceful and be on their way to hell.

A few years earlier, before the onset of her illness, she related a dream that she'd had. An angel came to her and told her she had nothing to fear, as she already had a place in heaven. When this story hit the church and the rest of the community, it was as if she had grown horns and become the devil himself.

"That was no angel that spoke to her!" someone with spiritual authority told me. I was told to dismiss her dream, as there was no way a heathen could take a place in heaven. Why were these beliefs leaving no room for someone as caring as this woman?

At her burial following the funeral service, I attempted to console a classmate and friend. She was so distraught. I told her, "Roxie is really, really ok. She went to heaven."

This statement got my friend's attention. She gave me a very mean stare and said "No she isn't! And you don't KNOW that!!"

I did indeed know that I was right. I had seen the tranquility. All was well with my mother's cousin on the other side.

CHAPTER EIGHTEEN

Upon graduating from high school, I took a trip to Georgia with my boyfriend and his family and then went to live with my brother and "sister" in Washington State. This move was made on motorcycle, as I needed very little in the way of belongings. I only stayed with them for four months. I was not eighteen yet and neither of them was my legal guardian, so I couldn't get a job. She and I would pick blueberries for cigarette money and we finally applied for food stamps. I didn't qualify, but she did, as she and my brother were not married.

Once I returned home from Washington, I worked for the little motel/grocery again. By early spring I was ready to move on. The winter was long and the only place to go for human interaction was the bar. By late January, I stopped going out all together. I seemed at peace staying home with my father and my little brother. After six or seven weeks of not going anywhere, I received a visit from the sheriff. In this small town everyone knew everyone so you were "friends" with everyone on some level. He recognized my "closed" emotional state and demanded that I be seen about town the coming weekend or he would be coming to get me. I went out, but I didn't enjoy it as I had before. What I noticed was that I could not look anyone in the eye. It took many weeks to able to communicate without discomfort.

After the snow cleared I moved in with my mother in the city and no longer attended church services. In the city there were several Lutheran churches. I just needed to choose one and start going again. I had received a couple letters reminding me to go to church. The letters gave a phone number for me to call to tell them why I had not been going. Up until that time I never knew that my parish reported attendance to a higher church authority. I felt like they knew too much about what I was or wasn't doing. Part of me wanted to go to church. On the other hand, I wanted to tell them to stop bugging me and stay out of my business. Who were they to tell me what I should be doing!?

A friend and I chose a Lutheran Church to attend. I thought that if I had communion there I might start attending regularly again. The pastor was at the door to greet the parishioners that day. As he took my hand he asked, "Are you an active member of another congregation?"

I answered, "Yes, but it's been a couple of years."

"I'm pleased that you are joining us today, however I will not be able to give you communion until you and I have a meeting." He was smiling the whole time. I think he was truly happy to see two young ladies come through the door without their parents in tow, but I was surprised that I could not take communion.

As I sat through the service, I thought more and more about his judgment of me. I had been going to the same church for eighteen years and I was being told that I couldn't participate at this one? Whatever happened to "Thou shalt not judge thy brother?" All I ever heard was not to judge others. How was it that he was doing just that? I was so disappointed that I never went back. Shortly thereafter I received another letter setting out that if I did not counsel with a Pastor in a certain amount of time, I would be excommunicated from the church.

All I needed was for the "Church" to threaten me. By the time I got this letter I had met my future husband, Rich. He had never seen me so agitated. I read the letter to him and added, "Excommunication!!! Thou shalt not judge thy brother! My Ass!!! That's all they're doing– judging me!!"

The final letter made it official–I had been excommunicated. I was relieved to be released from this group of people. I didn't want to be associated with hypocrites.

I had been to church with two friends, a Baptist and a Presbyterian. I was not comfortable with either faith. I was now "non-denominational." I didn't belong. I could no longer be labeled.

I feel like this episode was truly the first of many events that would take me through my evolution and metamorphosis.

CHAPTER NINETEEN

In the city I found work at a pizza restaurant, where I suffered an appendicitis attack on one of my shifts. I left an hour or so early and had surgery by morning. One week later, my boss called and demanded that I show up for work or I was terminated. I did not have the ok from the surgeon, but I was making a car payment and I desperately needed the money. All other waiters and waitresses took a break together, leaving me to tend to all the customers. By the end of the shift I was fired for not working at the pace demanded.

Losing that job was a very positive experience. Within a week after visiting the unemployment office, I was accepted into the CETA program. This program supplied education at the vocational technical school along with money for living expenses. I entered the computer processing program. I hated reading, so I was always behind on the literary part of studies, but the hands-on and general knowledge was very interesting to me. I did well, until meeting the man that would be my husband. I had to take an "incomplete" grade but received a letter of recommendation from the instructor. I felt guilty for using taxpayer dollars and not receiving a certificate of completion, but what I learned improved my ability to obtain work.

I was introduced to Rich by one of my friends at the Vo-Tech school. Our eyes met, I said "Hello," and that was that. We were together from that day forward until he was finished with this lifetime twenty-eight years later. I will never ever forget entering my friend's home, looking across the room, seeing him perched at her dining table holding a guitar. He was not sitting on the chair; he was sitting on the table with his one leg extended to the floor and the other resting on the chair, supporting the guitar. The introduction took place on a very pleasant evening the week before Easter. The three of us went out to the bar together and returned to her apartment. She fell asleep on a huge pillow she kept on the floor. Rich and I left and no one heard from us until the next week.

The moment we met I felt as if I had walked into a world of sunshine from a world that was dull and dark. It felt like the world was a beautiful new place full of light and life. It turned out to be like the Wizard of Oz; Dorothy goes from a dark, black-and-white world of terrible weather to a world of grand color and happiness, only to discover that this beautiful world also had a very dark and scary side to it.

When I was in his presence I *knew* that I was safe and protected and for the first two or three years my whole insides felt aglow. I had never felt that way before. I had been emotionally enthralled with two or three other gentlemen, but never had I felt the depth of all this emotion that came rushing into my life with Rich.

He had totally captured me by the end of the first evening together. He showed me respect, he protected me from a guy in the bar who was coming on to me, he kissed me with such passion I thought my head and body were going to melt. His touch was so tender yet it delivered so much strength. I couldn't bring myself to leave him that night--I had to stay with him--I never felt so wanted, desired and protected in my entire life. We couldn't wait to have sex and yes it was good (to put it mildly). He was eight years older and had had many women. He knew how to touch and where to touch, he knew massage techniques that could turn me into an animal–he was a master of sensual stimulation. He had obviously studied and practiced sexual arousal techniques.

He wasn't my first sexual encounter, but I had only been with one other man who even came close to knowing a fraction of what Rich knew about sexual pleasure. From the very beginning of our

66

relationship to the very end he would tell me daily how beautiful I was to him. I would often wake up to him softly staring at me. He would tell me that I looked like an angel and he just didn't want to stop looking at me.

We weren't very successful at dating unless you call two adults in heat "dating." We were so taken by each other that we couldn't manage more than one night apart. I began to live out of my car, staying with him most nights, but if his roommate wouldn't allow me to be there I would stay with Linda, the friend who introduced us. I don't think I ever slept in my car.

Within four months we had a place of our own because Linda met a love interest and moved in with him, which left her apartment available. We moved in before the ink on the rental agreement was dry with only a few kitchen items, a mattress, our stereo (eight-track player/record player) and our guitars.

He played guitar with ease. I struggled to play just a few tunes from a book that had a lot of popular songs. He liked to play jazzy/bluesy stuff, I liked the soft-rock/folk stuff. His playing came from within his soul, mine came from a book. He struggled to stay in tune when he sang; I could sing almost anything as long as it didn't go too high or too low.

After six months, we purchased a small trailer house (14x50) and found a place in the country twenty miles from town to park it. The landlord owned about fifteen acres and had two places for mobile homes in addition to their residence.

Late in high school I was strongly attracted to a guy with personality traits similar to Rich's. This guy had spent time in the service, stole alcohol from the local bar once, wasn't afraid to drive over the speed limit (way over), smoked pot and had an attitude that said "Life is good, I'm in control and I am going to get what I want. If I have to be patient and gentle for a long time I will. I can work hard if I have to, but I'd rather not. I'm too busy enjoying my life to let the little stuff get in the way."

I think I was attracted to "bad boys" because I never had any nerve to do anything that could be considered going out on a limb, let alone skirting the gray area of the law. And Rich was a bad boy.

Rich wasn't afraid of anything, worked really hard, but also loved to play on the other side of the law by driving fast, driving while drunk, doing illegal drugs, and enjoying life without worrying about what others might be thinking. I think I found it so attractive because I could be connected to wild behavior without actually doing it. I was safe from the trouble that could come from the behavior. I could watch it up close without actually doing it.

I tried marijuana during my senior year in high school, but would *never* possess any. I would check my clothes for any tiny bits of the plant before going home. I didn't smoke it because I liked the effects of the drug, I just liked being included in the group. It meant that at some level those people liked me.

CHAPTER TWENTY

It was the late seventies, unemployment was high. I was fortunate to be employed at the local Datsun dealership immediately following the end of the school year. I worked in the service department as the warranty clerk, shuttle driver and mechanic work-hours clerk. I enjoyed the work. I learned that a lot of men act very juvenile and that they were worse at getting involved with television soap operas than any woman I knew at the time. I also learned that most people were good souls, but some were absolutely ruthless. I witnessed an assault on one of the service-writers and was required to appear in court.

While working for the dealership I was in my first serious car accident. Driving the company vehicle, I was stopped for a red light and a car driven by a woman under heavy medication didn't even slow down as she came over the bridge and approached the light. There I was in the dealership's beautiful, brand new blue extended cab Datsun pickup. In an instant, the tailgate was pressed against the back of the cab and I had been slammed into the car in front of me and them into the car in front of them. Three of the four tires were flat from my braking and the force of the collision. I was so angry that someone could be so careless. I requested that she give me a dime to call my employer. She refused. I pressed, and she surrendered the dime. I received a serious whiplash, but no other injuries. The truck was totaled.

Then one day one of the regular customers asked me to consider changing careers. She worked for a title insurance company and thought I would fit in nicely. I talked to Rich; and we decided that I should interview with her employer. I was offered employment and two weeks later I was working as a receptionist/typist/delivery girl/accounts receivable and payable, recording clerk and secretary to the president/manager. The office consisted of five employees, so most positions were multi-faceted. My job was to do everything that the other positions needed assistance with. There were no computers and no fax machines. I learned how important it was to be exact in transcribing. Imperfections in information could result in an enormous monetary loss for the company. It was very interesting work and I enjoyed every aspect of my job.

After four years of being together, Rich and I discussed marriage and family. He had asked me to marry him after only one week of knowing one another, but we were both so worried that the infatuation and intense love from the moment we set eyes on the other would be a temporary state that we prolonged marriage for fear of dissolution. We both believed strongly in the eternity of a marriage commitment and didn't want to act hastily. Now after four years we accepted that we were truly not going to tire of one another and we were both ready to start a family. We went through the steps of acquiring a license. The license was good for six months. As the expiration date approached, we made an appointment with the judge for vows to be spoken--two days before the license expired.

Because of my husband's work commitments we were only allowed to "honeymoon" over the three-day weekend. We went to Eastern Montana to see his brother and family and stayed in motels instead of staying in their home. Forty weeks later our first son was born.

CHAPTER TWENTY-ONE

I continued my personal relationship with God at home. I had no other spiritual events worth remembering until I had Ray. I still find that experience so profound. There I was in critical condition on the operating table, and that is where I had one of the most awesome experiences of my life. I felt so good. Maybe it was one of those near-death experiences.

I clearly remember making the decision to stay on earth and not to go. It wasn't a difficult decision, but a very conscious one. I remember how totally at ease, joyful and just plain wonderful it felt-- wherever I was. I did not get the tunnel of bright light that so many people report, but the environment that I was in was beautifully lit. It was like natural sunlight, except that it was an absolutely pure, brilliant light. It felt wonderful to be in this light. Someone was there with me, but time has faded that part of the experience. The other person (or entity) was discussing my options with me and telling me I could make either decision – stay on earth or leave earth. This person was someone I trusted completely and was totally at ease with.

The combination of knowing that I was going to deliver a boy and having the exposure to the other side during the operation only confirmed for me that I was in God's graces. He still existed for me and was with me.

The pregnancy was fairly uneventful. I knew I was pregnant within hours of conception as I suddenly developed a case of claustrophobia. This lasted only one or two days. I suffered the standard first trimester morning sickness and then wanted to eat anything and everything in any combination. The only foods I became adverse to were undercooked chicken and venison –any venison. The wild game distaste came at a very bad time as a dear friend had just given us an entire deer as a gift and now we would have to wait to eat it or gift the meat forward. I recall managing to eat it if it was in chili, but I just couldn't eat it any other way and the smell was difficult to tolerate while I cooked it.

I was slightly underweight at conception, so I ended up gaining a total of forty-five pounds at full-term. I developed preeclampsia in the last few weeks, but I continued to work up until five days prior to delivery. According to the doctor's calculations, Ray was approximately one week late arriving. Rich had just gotten home from work and I was finishing a nice steak dinner when my water broke. We turned the oven off, put a plastic garbage bag on the seat of the pickup and covered that with a bath towel and off we went the twenty plus miles to the hospital.

It seemed like such a long time that I was in labor, but it was only hours. I remember how the contractions got very strong and very close together. None were painful. I was fascinated by the sensations. At around ten p.m. the monitor was indicating that the baby was under stress so they thought they would give me some Demerol so I would relax a bit. I remember clearly feeling the drug take effect as it entered my bloodstream and I didn't like not being in control. Very shortly after administering the drug the nurse called the doctor in to inspect me. I had developed a rash over my entire body. I was allergic to Demerol. The monitor was not indicating any reduction in the fetal stress, so a c-section was suggested as my life was now in the balance. As part of the reaction to the drug, my blood pressure had gone through the roof. The look of concern and urgency on the doctors' face was unmistakable. I was in trouble.

I was aware enough to know what time it was and requested that the delivery must take place before the strike of midnight as this was the first grandchild for my family and it was my father's birthday. It became extremely important to bring this new being into this world on July 6th for my father.

The doctor scrambled to get the team together, making no promises that he could make the deadline. The nurses hurried to ready me for surgery and off I went to the operating room. The anesthesiologist was there to greet me. He was very kind. He took the time to explain what he was there for and that in addition to normal procedures he needed to place an IV line in my neck in case I needed urgent attention during surgery. The pressure on my neck to "install" the IV was something that can still give me goose-bumps any time I recalled the event. I could not watch the movie "The Exorcist" for many years, as there was a similar scene in the fictional film. Just before sending me off to dreamland, the anesthesiologist and doctor asked me what I thought I would be having and I firmly said, "This is a boy."

They just laughed at me and said, "We'll see!"

At eleven fifty-seven our beautiful son was born.

I woke in the intensive care unit and was not allowed to see anyone, not my husband or new baby for twelve hours. It seemed like an eternity waiting for them to let me out of that unit. Ray was such a beautiful baby – all seven pounds and fifteen ounces of him. I remember all my visitors commenting on how young I looked – some even daring to say I looked like I was twelve. I was actually twenty-five.

He was the first grandchild for my family and the first male born in a generation on my husband's side. He was named after my husband's father, Raymond Thomas. I had a hard time accepting the "Raymond" part as it wasn't even close to being a popular name, but I understood the importance it held to my husband. I reluctantly allowed the name to appear on the birth certificate. I never had a problem with the name once we got home. Somehow he was indeed a Raymond. He was definitely a beautiful boy and healthy to boot.

I took the maternity leave granted by my employer. At the end of that period I gave notice that I would not be returning to work, as I believed that staying home with the baby was much more important. My husband supported me in my decision.

When Ray was eight months old, the title company called asking if I would please train a new replacement. I agreed when one of the employee's wives agreed to watch my son. I was still nursing and needed to have him close by. I could not have a sitter in my home as we lived twenty miles from town. I ended up working for another four months as each time I would train a replacement they would quit and I would have to start all over. When I trained the third one I advised the employer that I would not be extending my employment with them. Several times in the following years I was asked to return, but I declined. I enjoyed being a stay-at-home mom and the joys of motherhood I could not give up.

Ray began talking early and spoke very clearly. I remember that his first big word was hippopotamus. He would cry if I didn't buy him a banana or avocado when we grocery shopped. The only letter that gave him trouble was "s." He began walking at 11 months, fell a few times and gave it up until he was almost fourteen months. He was never a daredevil, always cautious and deliberate.

At seventeen months he quit nursing cold-turkey. I wasn't mentally prepared for him to stop and my body wasn't either. I was in such pain for days and I remember begging him to suckle. He had made his decision and that was that! He would lift my shirt, set his mouth to the breast and then turn away crying as he put my shirt back. I was amazed, hurt, fascinated, proud and relieved all at the same time. All the stories I had heard about how hard it was to transition a child from nursing to bottles and sippy cups was not going to happen for me. Not because I did something terrific as a mom. No, it wasn't about me. My child made the decision. He took control.

At about two and a half he started playing computer games. My husband had a portable computer from work and would load a game and Ray would enjoy manipulating the machine to his advantage. Many children play computer games now. It's difficult for many of us to remember how patient and knowledgeable one had to be to remember all the commands it took to bring a program onto the screen. Those were DOS commands. Ray learned them quickly and by three and a half he was pretty much on his own.

CHAPTER TWENTY-TWO

I became pregnant with our second son during Ray's second year of life and on June 21st, two weeks before Ray turned three, he had a little brother. We named him Patrick.

I had no pregnancy complications with Patrick. Again I gained forty-five pounds and again my water broke at home. Even though I really wanted to deliver vaginally, my body just decided four centimeters was the maximum dilation. This C-section delivery was not under medical emergency, so I was able to stay awake under local anesthesia. As soon as he was pulled from my abdomen I commented, "Oh . . . He's different!" The doctors in attendance replied that he was supposed to be. I didn't know what I meant, but I knew he was different right from the start.

I was twenty-eight when Patrick was born and visitors still commented on my extremely youthful appearance. Those comments were quite embarrassing at the time but as I got older (mid to late thirties) I learned to say "Thank you." I was thirty-nine the last time I had my identification checked to verify that I was indeed older than twenty-one, and yes, the clerk was very embarrassed.

On Patrick's eighth day of life, at approximately five p.m. he woke screaming. He nursed for only a moment and began screaming again. This went on the entire evening. By about ten p.m. he was getting quite sweaty. The poor little guy was getting all worn out. I called the hospital to ask what the symptoms of colic were. Those matched what I observed so I did the best I could to comfort him. By six or seven a.m. he was no better so I called to get him into the doctor as early as possible. We sat in the waiting room from eight a.m. until we could be seen. I don't think it was much more than forty-five minutes. As soon as the nurse saw him she called for the doctor. He was given oxygen and he was transported to the hospital across town. I drove over to be with him. That's when I learned that my infant had been in cardiac arrest. He was in critical condition and his blood sugar was almost zero. Seattle's Children's Hospital had been called and the air ambulance was on its way. I had enough time to go home and pack a few things. There would only be room enough for one adult so my husband made arrangements to take a commercial flight to Seattle.

I asked the neighbor who had eight children of her own if she could watch Ray for a few days. When I returned to the hospital Patrick was in a big plastic box and hooked up to so many things you couldn't see much unaffected skin. They explained to me that the patent ductus had closed and they had to administer medicine that cost the equivalent of my husband's whole month's salary for one dose. The drug would keep the valve open until he could go into surgery. The local hospital was extremely fortunate to have two doses on hand on that day.

Patrick and I were transported to the airport via ambulance and there we boarded the air-ambulance jet. I was in such shock. I couldn't say much. I was just trying to process everything. They had me sit at the back of the plane in a small seat tucked amongst the medical equipment and supplies. I could see the entire inside of the jet and was amazed at all the equipment and how they arranged everything so they could tend to the patient while in flight. The medical team frequently asked me how I was doing and if I needed anything to drink. I guessed I was fine – all I could do was nod that I was fine and shake my head no. I couldn't stand the thought of food or drink. My breasts were swollen and throbbing from the long hours since he last nursed, but I didn't really care. I spent the entire trip just watching every move of the nurses and pilot.

78

This was only the second time I had been in an airplane and this craft was a luxury unit compared to my first flight. This second ride however was more like something out of the "Twilight Zone."

Once we landed in Seattle the ground ambulance took us to the hospital with all the lights and sirens blaring. I was in such a strange world.

Patrick was taken away immediately. I was alone and simply had to wait. They would keep him as stable as possible until Rich arrived. As soon as Rich showed up they filled him in on Patrick's condition and immediately took the baby into surgery. The procedure allowed for closed heart vs. open heart, which meant they would not have to open and separate his ribcage to do the repair. It also meant far less stress to the baby's body. But even with the less invasive procedure, the cardiologist/surgeon did not think the chances of surviving were good. If he did get through it, his chances of recovery were fair.

So we waited some more. Frequently a nurse or doctor would come and update us on the procedure and his condition. Finally the surgery was over. We felt a certain amount of relief. We would be allowed to see him as soon as they were sure he was stable. The next time we were updated we were told that he was bleeding and they could not get it stopped. They suggested that we call clergy in to baptize him as they did not expect him to survive much more than an hour or two. Because I had been excommunicated from the Missouri Synod Lutheran church and my husband did not have an affiliation, we chose a Methodist chaplain to perform the rites.

It was so hard standing there with this tiny, lovely baby at such a critical moment. Were we really saying goodbye? How could it be that our baby had such a serious problem?

I think my first real test of faith was when Patrick went into heart failure and nearly died in Seattle's Children's Hospital. It was very difficult to go through all the waiting only to be told by the doctor that he was not going to live. I could feel such a heavy weight upon me. I felt like I was being crushed. Praying so hard in the little waiting room we were given brought a sense of solitude and privacy, but I can honestly say that I didn't feel any God presence. It was like I knew he was out there somewhere, and I was praying as hard as I could so he could hear me and get my message. Kind of like yelling at him…"LISTEN TO ME!!!! I NEED YOU NOW!! NOT TOMORROW OR IN TWO OR THREE HOURS. NOW!! RIGHT NOW!!!"

Then we were given a private room to wait the final minutes or hours. Rich and I each began to pray. I repeated the Lord's Prayer and Rich prayed silently, both of us offering to die so the baby could be spared. After a time we each stopped like we had been interrupted, looked at one another and asked if the other felt "that." Neither of us knew exactly what it was, but we both felt a sense of weight being lifted from us. As soon as we confirmed that we each felt the same thing, a doctor magically entered. He told us that for no reason that could be explained Patrick's blood had begun to clot and that it appeared he would not be dying this night.

I visited the hospital's chapel while I spent the weeks waiting to be able to take Patrick home, but I would only stay if I was the only one there. Most often I would just pray when I was in my room or while I sat beside his bed I would ask God to do his will when Patrick was having a bad day.

CHAPTER TWENTY-THREE

The stay at Seattle's Children's Hospital would be long. We arrived on June 29 and would not be going home until October. Patrick would spend all but seven days in the critical care intensive care unit. The bleeding that he experienced caused hundreds of small spots of damage on the brain that looked like pin-holes on the x-ray and post surgery he suffered severe swelling that caused even more damage. His poor little veins were poked every day. The nurses finally had to ask if I would allow them to put IVs in his head as they had no other places left until the veins had time to recover. He looked sort of cute with the cups protecting the cranial IVs - like a baby with two sets of ears – one set of skin and one set of plastic cones.

The hospital had just built a home to house families of hospitalized children. Within just a couple of days I was given a room. The home was just a few blocks from the hospital so I had no need for a car. Rich flew home and went back to work as soon as I was given lodging, so that Ray could at least have one parent with him.

The neighbor kindly became the full-time babysitter and Ray quickly became another family member to them.

Patrick was tested for Downs Syndrome, Cystic Fibrosis and anything else they could think of to try to make sense of his malady. My mother had been born with one eye and other relatives on her side of the family had birth defects. Patrick was born with one extra finger that protruded from the outside of his hand, just down from his pinky finger so they even did genetic testing. Nothing helped explain it. Patrick's extra digit had no bone, so it would not be a problem to remove, but it was way down the list of things to tend to.

I had only been alone with Patrick about a week when Rich came to visit with Ray so we could celebrate Ray's third birthday together as a family. It turned out to be a bit more than just the three of us as others in the "house" joined in. I cried every time I read Ray one of the books he had brought with him. It broke my heart that he would have to go and I would have to stay in Seattle. Ray and I both cried when he and his dad had to go back home. Ray was my precious one and I missed him so much. I wanted to live in both worlds but knew that Seattle was where I HAD to be as Patrick could die any minute. Ray was healthy and would be there when I returned – with Patrick or alone.

After approximately one month, Patrick's primary doctor demanded that I make arrangements to go home for a few days. He could not promise that Patrick would survive, but he did promise to remove the extra finger if I would just go spend some time with my firstborn and husband.

During the month of August I finally went home for about 4 days. Those were the longest days. I cherished every second that I was with Rich and Ray, but I could not concentrate on anything as I was always constantly wondering how Patrick was doing. I had become so familiar with the nurses' charts and I missed knowing what was going on. Every time I called the hospital I was assured that he was doing fine. Again we cried when I had to go back to Seattle.

Finances dictated that there would be no more visits until I returned home with Patrick. The phone bill however proved that loved ones had been separated.

I had made friends in the housing unit. Only a handful stayed the entire time I was there while many, many other families came and went. Most went home because their child improved, but a few had to go home alone. We made a wonderful support group for each other. Everyone was kind. One friend's son also had a heart defect; we had a lot in common. However, my closest friend was from

Venezuela. Their son was extremely ill and he would actually die and be revived every single week. While I was there they never diagnosed the illness. They could only treat him with their best efforts. Their situation made me appreciate mine.

Patrick had suffered brain damage from heart failure. There was no mystery, only the hope for delayed development that would be manageable. Hopefully one day he would be able to swallow and we could remove the "g-tube" from his stomach. This was the tube that all his food was administered through after he was no longer required to be fed intravenously.

A couple of days before Patrick was officially discharged he was sent "home" with me so I could learn to take care of him with nurses around. This meant learning to fold him into a blanket on a wedge of foam that would keep him securely in place. He could not lay flat as he would inhale any formula, called aspirating, and he would die. I learned how to administer the drugs he required and was taught how to clean everything correctly. I remember being so nervous I couldn't eat. I felt flush, a little dizzy and queasy every time we had an appointment with the doctors during those few days.

We got through all of that and went home on the airplane.

CHAPTER TWENTY-FOUR

It was wonderful to be home.

A couple of days later Rich brought home the German shepherd puppy we had contracted for and purchased long before Patrick's delivery date. The breeder was a friend and gladly held "Samson" the extra weeks until I was home to take care of him. The dog was gorgeous and well tempered.

We had a new life and the demands that Patrick brought were not easy for Ray to understand. He was a wonderful brother. He had been without me for so long; he just needed my attention and did his best to keep it for as long as he could. Sometimes the behavior wasn't exactly desirable, but he was only three and needed his mother.

The baby required feedings every hour, twenty-four hours a day. We saw the pediatric cardiologist three or four days a week. Patrick required hospitalization frequently, mostly for respiratory issues.

Just before Christmas Patrick developed seizures. The seizure drug he had been on since leaving Seattle was suddenly ineffective. Now we had to see the pediatric neurologist in town. He told me, "You should just put Patrick in the hospital and let him die there."

Let him die?! How dare he say that to me! I had learned a lot about Patrick's medical challenges from the doctors and nurses in Seattle and had created an amazing relationship with the local pediatric cardiologist, who allowed me to call him "Bruce."

So I asked this new neurologist, "Do you have any children of your own?"

When he said "Yes," I was blown away.

I told him how I could not believe any parent of a child could be so callous and make such a statement! We left that appointment and I immediately called Bruce, who made time to see me on the spot. I was so incensed that I was crying. I told Bruce what had happened and said there was no way in hell that I would ever take Patrick to that neurologist again. How would I know that he was giving Patrick life-saving drugs or therapy when he had such an attitude? Bruce had a working relationship with this other doctor and trusted him. Now he also questioned what the neurologist was up to. He arranged a meeting with the other doctor and reported to me a couple days later. Bruce needed to confirm with me that I had not changed my mind and he let the doctor know that his services would not be needed. He was fired.

CHAPTER TWENTY-FIVE

There were no other pediatric neurologists in our city or in any nearby town. Because of the severity of the seizures, Patrick was admitted into the hospital and the cardiologist made arrangements for Patrick to go back to Seattle's Children's Hospital for diagnosis and treatment.

On the day before Christmas, I was off to Seattle again. Bruce was not a neurologist and could not tell me that Patrick's seizures would not kill him. I was so nervous while I was waiting for the staff to get Patrick ready I nearly passed out. Oh yes, I had all the flushing and stomach queasies again. I was advised to eat a little yogurt. I choked down about three bites. Rich was running late and if he didn't get there we would miss our flight. I didn't need this on top of not knowing if the seizures would kill Patrick between now and Seattle. Rich finally arrived and got us to the airport. We were late but they held the flight just for me. The airplane was a prop-jet which could hold about twelve passengers—a "puddle-jumper." It was small, full of people and very, very loud. I remember being put in a wheelchair upon arrival in Seattle, but I sure don't remember the drive from the airport to the hospital. I was in yet another "Twilight Zone" episode.

Once again I was fortunate to be able to stay at the housing unit.

As soon as Patrick was seen by the neurologist, he asked me what I had been told in Montana. When I repeated what the neurologist said, he was aghast. He let me know that the seizures were commonplace and unless they became a lot more severe, there was no way the seizures would cause death. There was more concern over more brain damage than anything.

Patrick responded well to the new medicine, I was taught to administer the shots and we were allowed to go home on January 2.

Now there were more meds and more things to watch for and be concerned about. The 24-7 schedule intensified and continued. The only way I could keep track of what happened when and what needed to happen next was to develop a log or charting system similar to what they did in the hospitals.

To add to the stress, the bills from his first four-month stay had been coming in and we had no idea how we would pay them. We had sold the trailer and purchased our first real home shortly before conceiving Patrick. Now we had our mortgage, car payment and all the expenses of owning a home, plus the ten doctor bills and the outrageous phone bill we had racked up. There just wasn't enough money. I made arrangements with each provider to pay five or ten dollars a month until there was enough to pay more. All but the neurologist agreed to the miniscule payments.

Neurologic care was arranged but was now a two and a half hour drive from our home. This neurologist was a gift from heaven. She was someone who believed in the mysticism and the unknown of the brain. She offered a full chart of drug options, not just one or two choices. She was nationally well-known and highly recommended by the Neurologist in Seattle.

Hospital stays were still very frequent and by April Bruce was concerned that I would take Patrick and jump off the bridge. I was not getting enough rest and he could sense my frustration. I had never considered suicide, but I was definitely sleep-deprived. The most sleep I could squeeze in during a twenty-four hour period was three to four hours. I had been told of services available that would help with his care, but no introductions or appointments were ever made. I did not press because it was all I could do to be a mother to a normal child, a mother and nurse to a gravely ill child, a wife and a dog trainer.

Patrick was admitted into the hospital yet again, but this time Bruce would not release him for fear of putting me over the edge. Very reluctantly and gently he suggested that Patrick be institutionalized, as we could now tell that his development was almost non-existent. He would never function beyond a three to four month old. His heart was functioning nicely, but the brain damage was more severe than first estimated.

I could not imagine how I would ever abandon my child. An institution was completely out of the question. I demanded a "powwow" with all care providers. The meeting would be held in the hospital room. Ideas were discussed and applications opened.

Replies and responses came slowly. It was suggested that Rich and I get divorced so Patrick could receive Medicaid. That was also totally out of the question. How could all of these people think that destroying a family could possibly make things better? I said, "No way!!"

Research continued and it was discovered that there was a way to qualify Patrick without being a child of a single parent or a ward of the state. The application was submitted, and with a lot of support and paperwork from the medical professionals, Patrick became a Medicaid recipient. Our private insurance would continue to pay first and then Medicaid would kick in. Patrick had to be on Medicaid to qualify for other services. We were suddenly getting a feel for how the "system" worked.

When Bruce knew that all the services were in place and ready to go, Patrick was discharged. Once home, it took until almost October for all the government paperwork to be satisfactory so care could actually start. As part of the deal I was required to see a psychiatrist. I saw her twice and told her I wouldn't be back. She agitated me and didn't seem to care or have any understanding of my life. The only piece of good advice she had was that I was to dedicate 15 minutes every day to just me, not me and my older son or me and my husband. Just me. According to my log I could prove that there was not a fifteen minute window anywhere. I had no idea when I had 15 minutes in one block, but it gave me a goal to work on.

When care-giving services finally began, I had to learn to trust others to care for Patrick and document all meds, feedings, seizures, body functions and anything else that might be important. This would not happen quickly. I required that they log all important information on their shifts as I took it to every doctor appointment. For the first few months I stayed with the care-givers. At first they came once a week for four hours; just enough to give me a break. Then it expanded to a day care-giver and a once-a-week overnight stay. If the care-giver was in the home I just had one more person to worry about and I would lay there listening to make sure they did what they were supposed to do. It was quickly discovered that Patrick would have to go out of the home if I was expected to sleep.

The therapists, case-workers and caregivers were wonderful. Everyone was very supportive and gave me the time to make adjustments. We actually progressed to the point of going on outings with Ray. I was beginning to breathe. And I was finally allowed one full night of sleep every week or two.

Once I got Patrick home I had no time to think about church. I continued to pray, giving thanks for every day that he had given us Patrick and for all other things and people in my life. I was indeed very thankful for those in my life who provided support. There were many, many people. Some were only there for a second or two to offer a smile, hold a door or speak a word of encouragement. Others were there to help provide medical services. Still others were in my life to solely be my friend, whether casual or deeply involved, I was thankful for each one.

Why would God give me a baby with such a defect? Did I do something bad? Was I being punished? I couldn't think of anything in my entire life that might have been bad enough to receive this as punishment. I decided that there was no way it could be punishment.

Well then, what was it? Why did I have a baby that was nearly perfect at birth and then at eight days old a vegetable?

Somewhere around Patrick's turning twenty-eight months, Ray started asking when Patrick was going to die. I knew that Ray was well aware that he had been placed on the back burner and was no longer the focus of my attention. It broke my heart that Ray didn't want Patrick around anymore. I had no other option but to feed, medicate and care for the baby. Ray was good at entertaining himself and he loved playing games on the computer, so he wasn't difficult very often.

We had made arrangements for him to go to pre-school two or three days a week once it was determined that Patrick could withstand the germs, just not an actual illness. Ray also frequently played at the neighbors so he could interact with other children. He was now five years old and needed to develop his social skills. We had him tested for kindergarten and determined that waiting a year would be greatly beneficial. Going to pre-school was key to this part of his psychological development.

We lived twenty miles from town, but with going so often for medical appointments it was no trouble making the time for Ray's pre-school schedule. A friend managed the center and she was so excited when we registered him to attend. She reported that Ray was a delight to have around, he got along with all the children, but he had some trouble participating in group activities. His most traumatic day was the day they were creating silhouettes of each child. He absolutely refused to have his done, eventually crying due to the pressure the teachers exerted. Neither she nor I could ever get him to tell us why he refused. Her training told her that this was something to work on, as it had something to do with his self esteem.

By September Rich and I had decided that we would not want to have any more children if there was ever the possibility of bringing another disabled child into the world, so I scheduled a laparoscopic tubal ligation so that we could enjoy our tender moments without the fear of birth control failure. The procedure was performed on the day of our 6th wedding anniversary.

CHAPTER TWENTY-SIX

I had continued to "grow" into taking more time for me and had made the commitment to help Rich with his inventory on the evening of December 30 and all day December 31. Arrangements were made for Patrick to spend two nights with his overnight caregiver, Lola, and the neighbor would take Ray in while I was working. When Lola's time of arrival came near, Patrick began laughing with me. (He couldn't really laugh, like you might be imagining. He made no sound; it was all facial expression and body language). He was happier than I had ever seen him. He was rattling his wrist rattles and kicking his feet as I spoke and laughed with him. He laughed with me for a good ten minutes – right up to the moment Lola opened the door.

After working that evening and getting a decent night of sleep, I woke the next morning with a raging headache, so I called Rich and told him I was delaying my shift until I could get the headache under control. He had come home much later than I and went in quite early, as he had a lot more work to do than his helpers.

On December 31st at about 9 am the phone rang. It was Lola--and the paramedics. Patrick had stopped breathing while she was feeding him his breakfast. "Breakfast" consisted of tiny drops of formula thickened with cereal placed on his tongue while the full volume of nourishment went through the g-tube. The paramedic told me they were administering CPR and that Lola had also been administering proper medical care to him prior to their arrival on scene. I was to drive to the hospital where they were taking him. The emergency personnel had come from less than one mile from her home and the hospital only two miles away. I told the EMT that the hospital they were taking him to had never seen him and they needed to get him to the other hospital. They could not do that—it was too far away.

The roads were black ice that December morning. I called Rich and told him what was going on, then called the neighbor, dropped Ray off and drove the longest twenty miles of my life.

When I got to the hospital the staff didn't know me so they had to do all the formalities of taking my information. They also made me wait, which felt odd; the other hospital would have recognized me and let me right in to see him, filling me in on all the details as we walked. The wait seemed like a really long time, but I am sure it was only a matter of minutes. In that time Lola was able to tell me exactly what happened. She was feeding him when all of a sudden his eyes rolled up and his arms flung out. She had renewed her infant CPR certification one month before so I was confident that she knew exactly what to do.

As soon as a nurse took me in to see Patrick, I just looked at him, turned back to her and said, "He's gone."

There was no one home. There was a little body on the big bed, but nothing in it. I did not see any pain or discomfort from him--just a shell for a body. It was like when you find a cocoon and you peek inside only to find it empty.

"You little shit! You knew yesterday that you were going to leave! That's why you were laughing!" I don't know if anyone heard me or not. It didn't matter.

The staff asked if they could have my permission to discontinue CPR. I asked if they could just keep doing it until Rich could get there so he could be involved in the decision-making. I used the hospital phone to call him. He was there in ten minutes. I truly appreciated that the medical team was so sensitive to our needs. They had inserted a metal tube into Patrick's leg. When I asked what it was for they explained that it was to administer life-saving drugs if they could just get a pulse or heartbeat, which never came. I asked that they remove it or cover it up so Rich would not have to see it. It was so huge compared to Patrick's little leg and it looked so barbaric. I also demanded an autopsy. I requested that the body be cremated.

Through tears and shock we said our good-byes to our little "old man" on New Years Eve morning.

My Lutheran upbringing taught me that we receive punishment if God thinks we deserve it, but I was positive it wasn't punishment for something I had already done. So what was it? I was also taught that reincarnation was a concept that only heathens believed in. "There is no reincarnation!" Basically I was told that if I believed in it I was going to hell.

When people started saying that Patrick looked like a wise old man, I started wondering about reincarnation. I had been sensing something, but never realized what it was until someone actually said the words "wise old man." Everyone feels sorry for these kids because they aren't "normal" the way society wants them to be, but that doesn't mean they aren't happy. They are here for their own reasons that we cannot always understand.

Having this baby and having the weight suddenly lifted when Patrick almost died in Seattle made me wonder . . . is Patrick truly an old man in a baby's body? Through him I learned more than I ever imagined I could learn in a lifetime. That's what old people do, they teach the young people.

Later when I asked my friends what they thought of the possibility. I got more, "You just might be onto something," than total debunking. My friends allowed me to ponder the possibility.

I was never quite sure if I really believed in reincarnation until the day he died. I am convinced that his laughter during our last minutes together was his way of telling me he knew he was going. Yes, a wise old man who knew his time was up. I think another part of his message for me was to be happy. Why else would he have responded with more laughter when I giggled with him?

Rich went back to work so he could try to make arrangements with his staff to finish the inventory. I called my older brother who drove me to his house for awhile until I was ready to go home. We didn't talk a lot, but being with him, his wife and their infant son helped to bring clarity to my thoughts.

It was his wife's birthday and I felt very out of place. This was not right, her birthday was supposed to be a day of joy and celebration, not a day of loss.

Rich got home before I did and called me to ask if there was anything he could do. All I could think of was to have him remove Patrick's swing that we had hanging from the beam directly in front of the door. It would be the first thing I would see when I opened the door and I couldn't bear the thought. The swing that was used so often and meant so much to all of us would never hold him again. I would never strap him into his brightly colored therapy chair wrapped so invitingly in the net swing.

After a few hours I finally felt ready to come home. As soon as Rich and I gathered ourselves together and agreed how to tell Ray, we called the neighbor and she brought him to us. He knew something was wrong . . . he was very quiet. We sat down together and hugged him through our tears. I said, "Patrick died today."

Ray looked up at me and said "Good! I wanted him to die!"

I knew that he did, but I just didn't expect the honesty. Without hesitation Rich and I both assured him that it was okay to feel that way. We also made sure he understood that just because he wanted him dead, he was not the reason Patrick died. He said he knew that Patrick was really sick and he did not make him die. With that he went to play and left us in our grief.

This heartbreaking time was so simple to our five year old. He simply accepted what had happened. Wow! This created great pause for thought. It also somehow made the pain worse-- there were three of us in the house and only two in pain. I had to tell myself that it would be easier this way as there was one less wound to patch.

CHAPTER TWENTY-SEVEN

Bruce was out skiing with his daughter, so he did not get the message until later in the day. He was crying when he called me to find out how I was doing. He had become a family member to us and he too had lost a little one.

Calls were made to family and the following days were mostly a blur. It took more than a week to finally feel ready to make the necessary arrangements to hold a simple service. The funeral home was very gracious about holding his ashes for us. Eleven days after he passed, we held a memorial at the chapel and my sister-in-law's mother played the piano/organ. Her father, who was a preacher, gave the service. I actually got up and spoke and recited a poem I had been given. We did not expect so many people, and yet there were faces missing, like his occupational therapist and her team. They so wanted to be there, but had commitments they could not re-schedule. The funeral home director told me that he had never seen so many people at the service of a child of two and a half. I guess Patrick had left his mark on a lot of hearts.

Patrick made an impression on everyone he came in contact with. Every single person who was introduced to him commented that he looked like a wise old man. Now I was convinced that he truly WAS a wise old man. Why was he so happy the day before he died? He knew! The little turkey knew he was leaving!! What other explanation could there be for him to laugh when he had never laughed before? Every time I reflect on the short time of laughter I recall seeing a special tenderness from him. He was telling me something.

The autopsy did not discover any fluid in the lungs. There was no identifiable cause of death. Bruce deduced that it was a microscopic drop of fluid in his throat that had caused it to close down. Like when you get that sudden dry spot and just about choke to death (pardon the choice of words). Because Patrick did not have the ability to cough, he could not clear his throat. After thinking long and hard I could still not agree with his theory, as Lola and I had been feeding him for months and she was always very careful. I believe that he was going through a growth spurt and his brain simply short-circuited. It just turned off. Lights out. Patrick had indeed been going through a growth spurt. It matched more of what the caregiver reported than anything.

I couldn't help but laugh when I saw the Death Certificate reflect "Partial DiGeorge Syndrome" as cause of death. I laughed because of the stupidity and carelessness of the pathologist, but it made me *very* angry that a medical professional would list cause of death as Calcium Deficiency. That's all Partial DiGeorge Syndrome is. The body cannot assimilate calcium so supplements must be taken. Obviously the person responsible did not do their homework. They must have seen it listed in his records and decided it sounded like a serious ailment. With Bruce's assistance, I got a new death certificate ordered with cardiological/neurological complication(s) as cause of death.

Losing Patrick was extremely difficult. Even though I had known for two and a half years that he may not survive every day, the pain and grief was almost unbearable.

Progress was made slowly but surely. I took my time choosing the urn that would hold his ashes. The funeral home kindly held him all those weeks until I was ready. It was very difficult to find something that fit such a unique soul. It had to be tough and yet there had to be an element of a child's toy. I really had no idea what I was looking for. All I knew was that all the funeral home urns were NOT it. Finally, I had a local craftsman make a small cube. He crafted it of several different woods. The square was softened by rounding the corners. When they showed it to me, I cried. It was absolutely perfect. The artist in the man had captured my son. I was in awe.

In addition to the urn, the woodworker made a chest of the same woods where I placed the most cherished of Patrick's things that I could not bear to part with. Today it still contains the clothes that he wore on his last day as a mortal being, his favorite toys, the charting log, his first and last hospital bracelet and other special items. Because the chest was not made of cedar I can still smell him when I wish to re-visit; opening the chest and touching those precious things. These visits are less frequent. It's like scratching a scab – disturbing a healing wound.

I had been an active member of a support group for children with special needs during Patrick's last year of life. Our group was small, but we had become well-known for our knowledge and peer/medical community support. We produced a video for other parents of disabled children and their medical professionals. I alone had been approached by the director of the nursing program at the local University. Each semester one of her students was chosen to visit us for that semester. I enjoyed their visits and felt productive when I shared Patrick's medical condition and history. I was also asked to visit the class each semester, but did it only once after his death. I could not address the class again when I witnessed the entire room crying while hearing my story. I held and shed enough tears for all of them. The last thing I wanted to do was to create pain for someone else. When the director knew I would no longer present in person, she requested that I contribute to a nursing manual that she was publishing. I wrote a short story about Patrick for her. In exchange I received a signed copy of the manual.

In addition to the support group for parents of special needs children, I needed to join a bereavement support group. This came at the urging of the medical professionals who I had grown to love and respect. It helped me to feel not quite so alone, and yet I was very much alone. Not one person in that support group had lost a child with such special needs. Most of the families lost them at birth, to SIDS or by sudden accident. A tragedy, but nothing close to what I had experienced.

Very early in my grief recovery I discovered that I had no idea who I was. For two and a half years my identity had been "Patrick's mom." On rare occasions, I was lucky to be addressed by my given name. He had been my life twenty-four hours a day for two and a half years. Every breath I took was for him. Suddenly every responsibility I had was gone. Now I was just another person wandering the world. I felt totally lost and insignificant. The adjustment from saving a life every minute of every day to being a normal mom and wife was too much. I know this sounds strange because Ray was only five and a half, but he was so independent; he required virtually no care compared to Patrick. Life was normal and I hated it. Ray didn't need me as most five year olds do and that made my pain even worse. I knew I had not been the mother to him that he needed and should have had.

I experienced an enormous amount of personal growth in the short two and half years that Patrick was a mortal being. I learned that I could care for a child with severe disabilities. I could be an effective advocate. I could still be a mom and wife at the same time. I could operate on four hours of sleep. I could speak the language of the doctors and nurses. I was no longer intimidated by someone with more education or someone who was supposed to be in a position of authority. I could speak to them with confidence and ask the questions I had without fear. I finally felt like someone. If I had not had Patrick, I don't know who I would be today. Maybe I would still be a little mouse.

I never liked reading, but now at age thirty I finally began to peruse a few books. The nursing director, other mothers of disabled children, doctors, therapists and other parents in grief support group all made reading suggestions or gave me books as gifts. It was time to learn to read an entire book, enjoy it and get something out of it. One of the first paperbacks that I tackled was written by Elizabeth Kübler-Ross. It was called *On Death and Dying*. She told of her many experiences with children who had near-death experiences and how none of them were afraid of dying. Most of them told of God or drew pictures of God and things they saw on the other side. She wrote the book for families of dying children to help them cope and not be so afraid.

After reading that book I was even more certain that Patrick was a wise old man.

I don't know where I put the few papers I wrote after losing him. I was always very hesitant to write down anything that disclosed my true feelings after my mother decided to read my diary without my permission. The mouse in me found a safe place after that--I never wrote again until the pain inside was so bad that I had no other outlet. Crying was a release, but surely didn't express anything but "pain."

I wrote a letter to him after his first visit to me in a dream. Seven months had gone by before I had a single dream with him in it. When he began appearing in my dreams, he was always smiling at me and he was always content. My dreams would have me in situations where I hadn't fed him or given him any medicine for prolonged periods of time--weeks. I would suddenly remember that I should have been taking care of him instead of whatever else I had been doing in the dream. Embarrassed and in horror, I would approach him, expecting that I had caused him to be breathing his last breath due to my negligence. He was always in perfect health, clean and smiling as if to say, "Hi Mom! I'm so glad to see you again!!" I would wake up confused, but somehow comforted that he was never ever in discomfort in the dreams. In his mortal life he was frequently in discomfort.

So for five years after his departure, I mostly just pondered the reincarnation thing and wondered why God had chosen me to be the mother and caregiver. Why me? And why us? The two and half years he was with us affected all three of us profoundly. I felt so inadequate as Ray's mother. I had loved so much watching him learn; reading and playing games so I could watch his mind tick and see him blossom before my eyes. Keeping Patrick alive didn't allow me any time for that anymore and I was heartsick about it.

I could not pick up where we left off; he wasn't three anymore – he was now five and a half. Think about how much children progress during that period. It was gone for me; time that I did not get to participate in. I was in the house, living there. I could be touched and talked to, but I wasn't "there." It is so difficult to explain! I actually lost that time with Ray. The only choice I could have made to change it was to have put Patrick in a care facility, and pretend that he didn't exist.

I had also had a dream of Ray wandering out into the road and getting run over. And yes, he died in the dream. I woke up and ran to see that he was in his bed. Once planted, the thought of losing him was ever-present. One time he really did sneak out into the road, but the passerby stopped and called out to me. This only reinforced the fear within.

Now, after experiencing the death of one baby that had all kinds of problems and death scares, just the thought of losing Ray made me cry.

Grief is ugly, unpredictable and very, very painful. Simple things like opening a car door or doing the laundry would bring memories crashing into my head. There were no more burp rags, no more tiny little clothes and socks or receiving blankets. No more beeping machines. No more car seat, no more doctor appointments, no more stops at the pharmacy. I could not stop thinking of all those times when I would hold him as he was seizing, praying to God to make it stop or else just take him. I would be pleading to let him die in my arms and be at peace. My precious little baby. An hour could not go by without a flashing memory creating pain that cannot be described. Now he was gone and I felt so alone.

Rich and Ray gave me nothing but love and tenderness, yet they could not soften the pain I was feeling. Daytime was really tough, but getting to sleep was worse. That's the time our brains seem to want to share all the thoughts we have not allowed all day. It now became my time of crying and prayer--intense prayer for peace in my soul.

CHAPTER TWENTY-EIGHT

Life went on.

I had discontinued work in anything resembling a career path, although in Patrick's last few months I had been recruited to do occasional respite care for others. All my energy went to care-giving. Who was I? I had no idea. Because my most recent exposure was strictly medically-based, I was frequently asked if I was a nurse. I thought about going to college to become one, or maybe I would become a psychologist.

Rich was adamantly against my becoming a nurse because of his experience with his mother. It was indeed a fear of Rich's that, like his mother, I too would lose my sanity if I went into nursing. His mother was a very strong woman who "broke" from the constant exposure to death. It was so painful for him to have known what his mother was like before the depression and shock treatments, watching her change and become someone else. There was no way he would *ever* risk going through that again with someone he loved so dearly—me. He would not let me do anything that would take me away from him.

He did, however, support my idea of going to college. I struggled with what I wanted to be. I just knew I needed to be needed again. Going from twenty-four hours a day to the simplicity of raising a five year old seemed empty and meaningless.

I needed to experience the world outside of the medical establishment. I became a Tupperware dealer. I could control my exposure to humans and foster new friendships if I chose to, but most of all I wanted to develop my sense of belonging, feel as though I was accomplishing something and have something that I was committed to. Selling plasticware was not particularly rewarding, but it was so opposite of what I had been doing, it was actually kind of fun.

Ray entered kindergarten and loved every minute of it. He had a wonderful teacher and a small class of about ten. He caught the viruses that would be passed around, but we expected that, as he had been so protected the past three years. With the new relationships that school brought to both Ray and me, we began the slow process of evolving into a normal family again.

At that time statistics proclaimed that more than eighty percent of marriages with a disabled child would end in divorce. We were lucky, we were still together, but our marriage was a work- in-progress. A lot of work. Rich was a loving but complex man.

CHAPTER TWENTY-NINE

Rich grew up the eldest child of three. His brother was born when he was just ten months old and a sister came a few years later. His mother was a registered nurse and his father a refrigeration mechanic who worked as a civilian at the local Air Force base.

Before he turned eight he witnessed his little brother nearly burned to death: yes, they were playing with matches. His mother was beginning to spend a lot of time in an institution for the mentally ill. By the time he was a pre-teen, she had withstood more electric shock treatments than ever recommended. The treatments changed her dramatically. His parents would get into verbal fights ending with law enforcement taking his father away. This was a frequent occurrence even before her treatments for mental illness. As her illness progressed and she spent more time away, his father became the single parent and wage-earner, requiring him to work two jobs. Both parents consumed more alcohol than they should have, but he never labeled either of them alcoholics. The fights were usually, but not always, precipitated by drinking.

He and his brother were extremely close and referred to one another as "brother mean." Rich and his brother were only ten months apart and had very similar body types and strength. As they grew, their physical contests of boxing, wrestling, football and basketball were always well matched. Each would try to outdo the other. At the end of their contests they would tell each other how mean the other was-- hence "brother mean." Their respect and love for one another was unwavering. They would each do anything at any time for the other.

As for Rich's friends; he had very few casual friends. If he created a bond with another male, it was a bond forever and that friend meant everything to him. Only one or two of his friends from high school were still friends after he returned from Vietnam. He believed so strongly that if you couldn't trust the person who "had your back" you should never turn your back on them. I think he had that belief before his time in the military, but it became his life standard after he returned. I was not exempt from that standard.

Their sister was regarded as the baby of the family and the favored child. She developed severe asthma and this did nothing but exaggerate the attention she was already getting. The sibling relationships maintained those characteristics throughout my husband's life.

Rich began working by the age of ten, walking up to ten miles a day selling newspapers every morning. He grew up in eastern Montana where the wind blew almost constantly. Taking into account the wind-chill factor, the temperatures in the winter could easily reach sixty below zero Fahrenheit. His brother would occasionally join him in this work.

They lived on the "wrong side of the tracks," so he learned to fight early, as he would often be bullied on his way to and from school. His family did not live in a nice house and their mother would pick clothes out of the garbage on the streets for them. They would pay the price for their mother's shopping methods when they arrived at school and the children would recognize their clothes.

His heart was broken the day his father drove he and his brother to the local park to see their mother, granted a day-pass from the institution. He never forgot every detail of the where they were, what kind of weather it was, who was in the park, what the trees looked like that day, what she wore, how painted on her make-up looked, and the flaming red lipstick that was plastered all over her mouth. When they approached her, she lovingly hugged his brother, calling him by name, and then asked who this fine young man was. She wanted to know his brother's friend's name. It was Rich, her firstborn son, and she didn't have a clue who he was. He always tried to dismiss the incident, but it affected his relationship with his mother from that day forward.

He played football and basketball throughout school and had no trouble with his grades. By the time he was in high school he began to drink, sharing with me many tales of trouble and excitement. His favorite story was of "the car accident." He and three or four friends decided to drive as fast as the car would go the wrong way down the highway when an oncoming car forced them off the road. They hit a tree and rolled, completely totaling the car. He managed to get out and run home before the police showed up, but found that he could not move or walk the next day. He thought he had his father convinced that nothing had happened and that he was not involved in the accident. His father finally dragged him to the police station where he was interrogated, but was not incarcerated.

He enrolled in the Army, rather than getting drafted, and served time in Vietnam to spare his brother from being called to service. Despite his efforts, his brother ended up voluntarily joining a different branch of the armed forces as a medic. Rich refused to carry bullets in his rifle. He was what is referred to as a "conscientious objector." Because of his strong will, body strength and intelligence, he was constantly being asked to be promoted to officer. He always refused, which angered his superiors, so they would assign him the worst things they could think of as punishment.

Finally they decided to send him to the dogs because they were sure he wouldn't be able to handle the canines, and if they were lucky, he might even have to be discharged after a dog chewed him up. He actually excelled at dog training, receiving many awards and commendations. He became a mine-dog handler, which suited him wonderfully, responsible for saving the lives of others rather than taking them. He and his dog would walk in front of the troops to identify any dangers, including people and explosives. He tried everything he could to take his dog home with him when he was finished with his enlistment—to no avail.

Drugs were readily available and he learned which ones he liked and didn't like. I have often heard that a soldier on the front lines will either chose religion or drugs to deal with the stress—Rich chose drugs. The religion was there inside him; you just had to dig down to get to it.

Upon returning to the States, he was ridiculed and spit upon for being part of the conflict; as most Vietnam veterans were. He had learned to not trust any media reports or any politicians. Many things happened in Vietnam during his time there and reports were complete fabrications; nothing close to what was really happening. As many articles and documentaries have disclosed, more servicemen died after they returned home from Vietnam than were lost in the conflict. Rich lost many, many friends from suicide or "accidents" after returning home. Somehow he managed to stay sane, hold a job and get on with his life. The only time he would smile while discussing Vietnam was when he would recall just how close he was to being in the same unit with Jimi Hendrix—he missed serving with him by only weeks. Only on rare occasions would he speak of his military service.

It took Rich many years to lose the drug habit but the alcohol was a constant presence. He could never have just one or two drinks. If he had a drink he drank until he could hardly walk. He did manage a few months of sobriety at different times. He never ever drank during work, but as soon as he was done. He had a small group of very, very close friends, but they too fought the same alcohol demon. He spent a great amount of time with them after work and on weekends.

Rich always dreamed of owning his own business. He began by obtaining jobs with small business owners learning everything they could teach him. His first job was at a tire store, then a small semi-truck dealership and finally a larger truck dealership.

I met him when he had been with the larger dealership for about two years. Shortly after that, he was offered a department manager position, the youngest person ever offered the position. They had been through ten managers in seven years, so they thought they would just put another warm body in the chair until they could find an experienced person to take the job. He was determined to prove them wrong, and he was a great success. His work and customer relationships meant everything to him and the company's numbers proved it.

Computers were just beginning to find their place in the small business world, so Rich made it his business to learn how to use them. He nearly lived at work for two months until he taught himself enough to be able to run the business with the new technology. There were no classes or instruction offered, just the demand to make it work or lose your job.

He was passionate about his career and totally dedicated to his work and friends. He was the happiest when he had business problems to solve.

Because of his preferred schedule, I had to learn to accept that I would not see him until nine or ten p.m. each evening. When he attempted sobriety, we had a lot more time together because he could not go to his friends' homes after work. Most often he would be with his friends "winding down" and having a few "pops." I never understood his excessive drinking and he never understood why I got so worried, angry and upset when he would finally stumble through the door. Even after a couple of serious car accidents, he still didn't understand my pain about his drinking. If it was after seven p.m. and he wasn't home I worried whether he would make it home at all. He was extremely lucky never to be convicted of a DUI or cited for reckless driving. The only attempt at charging him with a DUI happened when he was on his way to a friend's home immediately after work. The charge was dropped. His drinking problem created most of the problems in our relationship.

Once Ray started talking and became more engaging, Rich came home a little earlier a couple days a week and spent a little more time at home on the weekends. He had taken up golf as part of his "management obligations," so that was just another of his dedications that did not include family.

As Ray grew older, I discovered how intelligent my husband was as I listened to their interaction and discussions. I knew that Rich could do any business math in his head and could create a spreadsheet or computer program for whatever application he needed. He understood the stock market, and also astrology, music, engineering, mechanics and quantum physics.

He loved playing guitar. He preferred the blues and always said, "You can't PLAY the blues unless you HAVE the blues," although he also had a great appreciation for The Beatles. His favorite artists were Muddy Waters, Billie Holiday, Eric Clapton, Jimi Hendrix, Janis Joplin and Stevie Ray Vaughn.

Rich's father taught him how to cook, so frequently he would take on the task. It was always very, very good.

He was very learned, passionate, sensual, creative and extremely sensitive. He loved hard, played harder and never ever tolerated teasing. He was incredibly dedicated to his work and providing for his family. He taught me to say thank you (honestly, I was never taught to say it as a child). He also showed me that I could be proud of anything I accomplished. Without him, I would have remained a mouse. He nurtured me and brought out my self-confidence and self-worth.

Because of his intensity, he could become extremely angry and his words could cut a person to ribbons. His daggers went deep. In his anger he would repeat things I said or did years before as if they were indiscretions from the current week's events. I suffered from a major inferiority complex my entire life and this did nothing but reinforce my inadequacies. If he was grumpy, I got quiet. The few times I spoke, I ended up fueling the fire, so I learned not to speak until he was no longer angry or upset—usually that meant when he had finally passed out. If I had to speak, I would say only neutral things that would not increase his anger. Of course this didn't always work. Sometimes my non-response would only intensify his sense of frustration.

I find it very difficult to describe Rich without making him sound like a rotten husband. I know he loved me dearly, but he was very complex and was not home much to help me care for Patrick and Ray. I would have to call his friend's homes to find him so I could tell him I was taking Patrick to the hospital. The challenge he faced with alcohol created so many difficulties for us. In the end, he was a wonderful person and I loved him very much. I would not be who I am today without those stressful but wonderful years together.

CHAPTER THIRTY

As the years passed, I found that I was actually afraid to get as close to Ray as we had been before Patrick. I really didn't notice it until friends would ask things like: Do you hug him much? Why don't you say "I love you" to him when he goes somewhere? Ouch!

Ray had developed independence and I had developed fear of loss. We were still very close and loved one another with all our souls, but we rarely expressed it physically or verbally. Each of us had a look that we would give the other, the little eye twinkle, so we both knew what the other was saying.

Rich had told me when we were first dating that he would smother me with affection. He was always very affectionate, and yes, at certain moments in time I would reject his affection, but he never gave up on me. I thank God for that to this day.

Because we lived in the country, the local school was small and Ray developed wonderful friendships with all of his classmates. His first grade teacher immediately identified his excellence in math, art and science, but could not offer him advancement because there were no programs available until fourth grade. Even with no challenges for him in these areas, he loved school, his teachers and classmates.

Ray was always "thick" statured. When he was born, he weighed in at seven pounds fifteen ounces. He felt like he was filled with lead. This never changed. So as life goes in school, there was a student who loved to give him a hard time about being a little bigger than everyone else, even though he wasn't fat. This child taunted him for more than a year with verbal and physical assaults when finally one day Ray had had enough. He reached his hands out and put them around the other child's throat. Of course, the other boy ran to the teacher. I received the call to have "a meeting." What could my precious little boy have done to require a meeting with the teacher?

With Ray present, the teacher explained the incident to me and the required disciplinary action. Ray was asked if he was sorry he choked the other child. He so matter-of-factly said "No, because I didn't choke him! I only put my hands on his throat because he deserved it!" It was all the teacher could do to keep a straight face. She knew the other child had been taunting Ray, but had not been able to witness and intercede before the incident. Ray's disciplinary action was to tell us that he wouldn't do it again. The other child was required to apologize and write a paper.

Rich finally decided to teach us how to play golf. We always enjoyed our time on the course. Ray would mostly just putt, but he had a great time driving when people were golfing slowly enough to allow him time to swing his clubs. Rich taught me to fly fish very early in our relationship so we also did a lot of fishing on the creeks and rivers in our area. We rarely kept what we caught. We were doing it more for the pure enjoyment of being in nature.

Rich purchased a four-wheeler and made rugged trips out with business associates. Soon after, he purchased another one for me. We were fortunate that we could leave directly from the house and not have to haul the vehicles in the truck to take a ride. As soon as we drove out of the neighborhood, we were on a logging road that took us straight to the mountain peak. Near the top where a small stream trickled through the trees, we would park and just listen and take in every element of our surroundings.

CHAPTER THIRTY-ONE

Something that Ray and I enjoyed doing outdoors was picking huckleberries. It was a family tradition for me that I continued now that I had my own family. It required a bit of driving to get to the patches that produced an abundance of the sweet fruit because the ones I was familiar with were sixty miles away. Usually I would drive the hour to see my younger brother and his wife and/or my parents and make a family outing of it. We would pack water and sandwiches and venture off to our favorite places. These spots were somewhere between thirty minutes and an hour from my parents home and ninety percent of the travel was on logging roads. The huckleberry season was fairly short – only two to three weeks at best. It would usually take two hours of serious picking to get one gallon of the precious berries. They were much too expensive to buy from the folks who figured out ways to harvest them much faster. I always preferred picking them myself. There was just something special about hand-picking every precious fruit.

I wasn't always able to make the trip to my home town so I would always kept my eyes peeled for berry patches whenever we would go for drives in the mountains for fishing or sightseeing. Eventually I found patches much closer to home.

One summer my older brother, his wife and their two-year-old son joined us on a day of picking. We had a wonderful time. I needed to get back home by early afternoon so we picked right up to the last minute. As we were on our way back down the mountain on the dusty single lane logging road, without any hazard or warning, the steering wheel jerked out of my hands, making the car turn ninety degrees to the left. Oh my God! In an instant we were headed off the road! On the right side of the road was a cliff, the left side was a drop-off. I had both feet pressed down as hard as I could on the clutch and brake. The car stopped after we broke through the small mound of soil that defined the edge of the road. The entire front end of the car hung over the edge of the cliff. All I could see was air, and as I looked down I could see the tops of trees well below us. We were all so frightened to move, we just looked at one another for a moment and asked, "Now what?"

How did we get out of this little pickle? My brother very carefully crawled to the back of the car. He stood on the back bumper until his wife and the two boys were out. After an attempt or two to back up, I got out. Reverse was a futile effort in a front-wheel-drive car when the front tires were hanging out there in thin air . . . not touching a thing. We found a couple of small logs that we were able to lodge under the front tires. This gave them traction. Every move we made was with great care. None of us were prepared for the long walk back to the highway, and we certainly didn't want to create a situation that would send the car down the hundred foot fall. After getting the car back onto the road, we spent a short time walking back to see if there were any large rocks protruding from the road that may have hit the axle. We found nothing--only our religion.

CHAPTER THRITY-TWO

My Tupperware selling days lasted about a year and a half. The social workers who had provided and coordinated services for Patrick approached me to work full-time with disabled adults. Although my expertise was with an infant, I was not comfortable dealing with other special-needs children. I found that doing rehabilitation training and general housework for adults suited me fine. I had randomly worked a few jobs while Patrick was still living so the social workers pressed for me to do more now that I needed income and had the time. During my "social adjustment period" I continued to work a few hours a week with the disabled. I gradually added to my schedule until I worked every day from about nine a.m. to two or three p.m. This allowed me to be home when Ray got on and off the bus before and after school. It felt good to be giving back to the system that served us so well when we needed it. The income was greatly needed and I really enjoyed my friendships and associations.

Occasionally Ray would be home alone for thirty minutes to an hour after school. He knew he could call the client's home or go to the neighbors. Having a very protective German shepherd dog kept all of us at ease during these "home-alone" times. He had shown interest in cooking so I always let him help me in the kitchen whenever he wanted to be involved. One day when he had gotten home before me, he greeted me at the door, saying he had a surprise for me. He presented me with a plate of carrots, celery, cheese and peanut butter and told me there was more. He was glowing with pride. He had baked a batch of muffins, using the only cookbook I owned that had no pictures. The recipe he found required the muffins to be rolled in melted butter and cinnamon and sugar as the final touch. I had never made the recipe before. They were done to perfection and I was amazed. He was nine years old at the time. He was so proud! I was in awe and my heart gets all warm and glowing to this day remembering it.

CHAPTER THIRTY-THREE

By the time Ray was getting ready to finish third grade, Rich was approached by a close business friend from Boise to join his dealership as the department manager in their satellite store. He had been offered many jobs over the years from every part of the country. None of them offered a management position in a small, one-light town that still had the hometown community feel.

Rich had not been treated well by his superiors after Patrick died. The inventory numbers did not come out correctly the year of his passing and they never let up on him. They did not give him a chance to deal with his grief. They showed no compassion after Patrick's memorial service and he was very hurt by their actions. They had even threatened to discharge him.

The associate in Boise was fully aware of these events. The new job would mean moving out of Montana. This was a big decision. With the exception of birth to five, I had never lived outside of the county where I was raised. Rich had also lived ninety percent of his life in Montana. Somehow the opportunity felt right, so in April we took a short trip to look over the Idaho dealership and surrounding area. Rich accepted the position and began working for the new dealer-principle on the first of July.

During our last full year in Montana we had sired our German shepherd out for breeding. The stud fee was the pick of the litter, so we now had two male German shepherds. They were both beautiful dogs. Now we would have to arrange care for them while we were gone. We kenneled them in a boarding facility for the short trip in

April, but it would be far too expensive and stressful for the dogs to board long-term while we found a home in Idaho.

During July, Ray and I had made the trip to Idaho to see Rich and explore our new hometown, getting a feel for what it might have to offer. I inquired about the banking options and employment opportunities for me. I found everyone especially friendly and kind. The banker mentioned the school for the deaf and blind and there was a home for the disabled in town. He also referred me to the title company, so I took the opportunity to pay the manager a visit to talk about possible employment. He just happened to be available when Ray and I walked in. We visited for about an hour and a half and by the time I had to go, I was assured an entry-level position. A start-date had not been set, but I would be notified as soon as the current entry-level person went back to school. Just like that I was employed! I was thrilled. I never expected to get a job so easily. It had now been ten years since I last worked in a title company, but I looked forward to that type of work again.

Rich made no secret that he was glad that I did not continue my health-care related work. He would tell me, "Nobody dies in business." For him there was always the underlying fear that I would go crazy like his mother did if I continued to work with people who could die at any time.

We advertised our home for sale and did the fix-its, painting and touch-ups before Rich left for Idaho. There seemed to be a lot of interest in our home, but no solid offers. It was soon the month of August and Ray and I would have to move to Idaho before school started, so we contracted with a real estate agent and hired one of the neighbor's young adult children to housesit. He had been one of Ray's babysitters, so he was familiar with our home and the dogs. As a young man, it gave him his own place to stay without paying rent, so it was a good arrangement for all of us.

As part of the package, Rich's new employer agreed to pay for a moving van. We didn't pack anything as we would be voiding the moving company's damage warranty if we did. The packing would be left for them to do. So, off we went to Idaho to be with Rich shortly before the school year began. He had been staying in a motel room, so we simply joined him there. He was house hunting, but had not found anything that he wanted to make an offer on. He was glad we were there so that we could now look at homes together.

We were all happy to be a family again. It had been so hard saying goodbye and watching him drive away, knowing he wouldn't be there for the fourth of July or Ray's tenth birthday. Both occasions were special days for us. This year was different.

The move to Idaho was somewhat spiritual in that neither of us understood why we were supposed to leave the place we called home and the state we both had lived in for more than thirty years, and yet we each knew we were being guided to relocate. So we didn't fight it; we moved.

Rich told everyone that he needed to get me out of the house and reminders of Patrick. I just told people that Rich needed a fresh employment group. We both said, "If it doesn't work out we can always come back, but if you don't try you'll never know."

When August rolled around and Ray and I had officially moved into the little motel room in Idaho, I was only unemployed for about two weeks. I was able to walk to and from work as it was only about five blocks. When co-workers would say, "Good-bye, see you tomorrow. I'm going home," I would laugh and say, "Ok then, I guess I'll go to my room." There was only one bed, so Ray had to sleep on the floor—and no, he wasn't thrilled about that arrangement. There was no refrigerator, microwave or kitchenette; only the main room with the bed and television, and the bathroom. Our closet consisted of a suitcase on the floor and a single rod that was no more than twenty-four inches long for our nice work clothes. There was a diner across the road and a grocery store a block away that sold hot deli chicken, cold cuts and a small variety of prepared salads. Our "refrigerator" consisted of a medium-sized cooler with ice so that we could keep some milk and juice on hand along with any left-over salad or chicken. Obviously, we had to purchase ice every day. I think the room had the standard coffee maker, but I don't recall using it much. Rich and I got our morning coffee at work.

CHAPTER THIRTY-FOUR

Finding a home was not as easy as we had thought. Our home in Montana was not selling as quickly as we needed it to. Being so far away made it difficult to negotiate with our real estate agent and any prospective purchasers. Weeks went by. On one occasion I received a phone call from my agent and I simply broke down crying right there in the middle of the office. She made me very angry and I threatened to get an attorney if she did not start doing her job. With all the interest we had prior to listing the home, we were very confident that she could get the house sold without any trouble. She just wasn't getting the job done. Even if we did find a home in Idaho, we couldn't buy it if the house in Montana hadn't sold. It was frustrating.

We promised to have Rich's mother live with us, as we had not been able to relieve his brother of her care while we were in Montana. So the home we were looking for would have to be large enough to include mother-in-law space.

Ray was involved with the house hunting as much as Rich and I. As we would drive around and refer to listing documents, Ray would repeatedly mention that we should look at one certain home. It was about five miles out of town in a very small subdivision and it came with a touch over two acres, with an additional two plus acres available for purchase. The exterior design of the house was not attractive to me at all. It looked as though it was two halves that had not been matched properly. After many weeks of searching, Ray and the real estate agent made me promise to just go in and look. Ray just kept saying "Mom, We HAVE to look at this house! This is the house! I don't know why you won't even look at it!" So I reluctantly agreed.

Up the stairs to the front porch we went. The real estate agent opened the door and Ray and I entered. It was gorgeous—high vaulted ceilings, large open rooms with lots of windows, a large kitchen, formal dining room, formal living room, a family room and a rec-room in the basement--all this with three bedrooms and a master suite upstairs with two additional bedrooms in the finished basement. The master bedroom had two closets, one nice big standard one and one large walk-in. The walk-in closet was only about one foot smaller than our entire bedroom had been in the trailer. Not only did I love the home, this floor plan could accommodate a mother-in-law. Ray beamed from ear to ear and was justified in saying "I told you so!" He reveled in my joy and excitement.

When people walk into the home that will be "the one" they know it instantly. There is no "I like it but . . . It's just, "This is IT!"

This was now the second home Ray had picked out for our family. Rich had taken him along when he searched for our first stick-built home. He always told me that Ray had chosen the house, and I always assumed that he was joking and just trying to make Ray feel like he had something to do with it. Now Ray was telling me that he had indeed picked out the house when he was just two and a half—and now this one. It brought back the memory of my first walk-through in our first real home; Ray running around, pulling me into each room to show me the beautiful house. We asked him which bedroom was his and he immediately claimed the master bedroom. Of course, we had to disappoint him.

This home had more spaces for him to claim. He was now ten years old and knew that there was no chance of him claiming the master suite. He may have joked about it, but he had other rooms in mind. Each of the bedrooms was a different color: one was blue; blue carpet and wallpaper with blue flowers and stripes - another was green (pea soup green); yes it had green carpet and the walls were basic white with very bold, broad green stripes with an arrow that pointed around the room. And, finally, a pink room; pink carpet and lots of flowery wallpaper. The only bedroom with neutral color was the master bedroom. However, this room also made a statement with its huge blue and brown flowered wallpaper, cedar fence paneling and pale blue sheer curtains. It was quite obvious that the previous owners' children were all girls.

We finally got a buyer for our home in Montana and the ownership changes came in late October. After four long months we would be able to move out of the tiny little motel room.

Suddenly we had to deal with all of our belongings in Montana. Rich had been trying to negotiate with his new employer to pay for both the motel rent and the moving van, but when all the numbers were crunched the employer said "one or the other." The motel room ended up being the larger of the expenses, so we would have to get up to Montana and pack everything ourselves, rent a U-Haul and get back to Idaho as quickly as possible. Neither of us had vacation time available and couldn't really afford to take days off without pay. To this day, I don't know how we did it, but we packed, cleaned and moved everything we owned in four days. Yes we were exhausted, but it was done.

In Idaho we helped the seller pack and move out so we could move into our new home on October 29.

Poor Ray, even though one of the rooms was blue, it was still very feminine – no masculine elements at all. The pink room had the most space and nicest design, but how could he ever have friends over if he lived in "the pink room?" He decided he could live with it until we had a chance to de-feminize it. Taking down the flowered wallpaper helped a lot and a couple of area rugs hid some of the pink carpet. He also put a skull and cross-bones flag on the wall above the bed to help keep eyes up off the floor.

On October 30th Rich's brother arrived with his mother—at 9:30 at night. They were gone by 7 am the next morning. We had had no time to put anything where it might belong, so we hurriedly arranged a bed for her to sleep in that night.

CHAPTER THIRTY-FIVE

Adjusting to living in a huge home after the tiny motel room was a pleasure. Adjusting to living with mother-in-law, her bird "Tweetie" and our two dogs who forgot they had ever been house-broken was a whole different matter.

"Mother" had always lived in communities where she could walk to the store or call a cab. Now she was five miles from the nearest "convenience." Every day she would call me at work asking any question she could think of, or making a request for me to take her somewhere or pick up something at the store. It made it very difficult to be effective at work when she always had me wondering what the heck she was up to at the house.

I knew that Rich did not trust her, and within a couple weeks she began making up stories about a woman that would call for Rich, wanting to see him. She also wanted the existence of this mystery lady to be kept from me so she would always try to tell him secretly. We did not understand why she wanted the drama of "another woman" to be part of our lives. She had done similar things to Rich's brother and his wife, but they were somehow able to humor her. Rich found no humor in her ploys and was very firm with her about it.

Rich and his mother had always been at odds and they could push each other's buttons without any effort. Needless to say, tempers flared early on between the two of them.

Ray was not immune to Mother's games. She constantly reminded him that he was "fat" and basically told him that everything he consumed was not good for him. She was convinced that the organic nutritional supplements and snacks that he enjoyed were actually destroying his health. She would also tell him things that the "people" in her head or the "radio" in her head were relaying to her. The FBI and Secret Service were her constant companions. She was not a person who could sit still or be quiet, she always had something to say or do; always talking to "someone"—real or imagined. The talking never stopped— even during the night when we were trying to sleep. It drove Ray crazy, as his room was right next to hers.

On one occasion, we took the chance of leaving Ray and Mother alone for an overnight trip. It was the first company Christmas party for me, and we could not bring Ray. We had not lived there long enough to ask a friend to take Ray in for the night, so we left the two of them home with the dogs. We came home early—and thank goodness we did! The house temperature was ninety-eight degrees. Mother had set the thermostat at its highest point. We asked her, "What do you think you are doing? Trying to burn the house down?" She firmly stated that Ray had done it and she didn't know what we were talking about. Ray always preferred cool room temperatures and he knew never to touch the thermostat. Reasons were piling up to worry while she was home alone.

Ray was ten years old but he had never been around people who argued and raised their voices at each other every day, and he certainly had no idea what mental illness looked like. Up until now he knew that Rich would speak loudly or voice his displeasure, but we never argued or fought. He had never experienced such stress.

Living with Mother wore thin quickly. None of us wanted to go home after school or work. Ray would come to my office whenever possible and just quietly wait for me in the break room. Rich already knew to find solace with alcohol. But now, for the first time in my life, I began to have a drink when I got home each night. Rich would drink to pass out as soon as possible so he could avoid engaging her,

132

and I began to drink to soften my mood so I could tolerate her and the constant verbal abuse between she and Rich until he did pass out. Ray would just try to hide in his room or stay near his father. Rich would always verbally protect and defend us.

As much as we wanted to stick with it and take care of "Mother," we simply could not. At the end of three months we told her that if she didn't buy a plane ticket back to Montana, we would be sending her there against her will. There was no way we would consider driving her back, as the road trip would be much too long. We had HAD it-- we felt we might even stop alongside the road, push her out the door and abandon her. It would have been eight hours of bickering and threats of harm.

Rich and I were disappointed in ourselves that we could not carry through with our commitment, but we also knew that we would harm someone or disintegrate as a family if we continued. What his brother had done for years we could only do for weeks.

Mother went back home, and we assumed life as a happy family again.

CHAPTER THIRTY-SIX

After Mother left, we finally started feeling like the home we purchased was ours. She had a way of living in the entire house. We had no sacred space to call our own. We finally bought furniture for the formal living room and dining room now that neither she nor her little cockatiel would be soiling new furniture. The house was a comfortable, welcoming place.

Ray made many friends quickly in our new hometown. I loved my job, my co-workers, and found everyone in the community especially friendly.

Ray was old enough to be involved with Boy Scouts instead of Cub Scouts, so we contacted the local leader. To our surprise, they had also recently moved to the community and were just starting the Methodist Church sponsored troop. Other churches sponsored scouting, but we did not belong to any denomination and knew that the Methodists would not pressure the boys in their faith as the others were known to do. Ray and two other boys (Jack and Jason) were the founding members of the troop. The membership grew and he enjoyed all that scouting had to offer. He loved the leader, the camping, outings and service projects. He earned the nickname "Ralph" because he was throwing up every day of his first summer scouting camp.

Ray had only been away from us once before joining the Boy Scouts. The first time was when he was seven. Two years after Patrick's death, Rich and I went on our first vacation--a float trip on the Hell's Canyon with his friend from Boise. It required us to be gone for five days. We left Ray with my younger brother and his wife. He spent the better part of all those five days crying and vomiting from separation anxiety. Three years later would be his second attempt at being away from us. He was determined to stick it out with his fellow Boy Scouts even though he felt so nauseous. He did fine, spending a single night with a friend in the same town. It was a whole different thing being many miles away for a week.

I suspect it stemmed from all the time that I had to spend away with Patrick. Somehow inside his darkest fear would be that I wouldn't be there when he came back.

The office I worked in was directly across the street from the Historical Society, so Ray made a point of exploring the museum and getting to know the folks who ran it. Before we knew it, he announced that he had a job—volunteering. He was the youngest person the board had ever approved to volunteer and they were thrilled.

We had been warned that Idaho schools lagged behind surrounding states and that he might be bored the first year. Sure enough, halfway through the school year I noticed that his grades had dropped dramatically, so I made an appointment with his teacher. She thought that he was doing fine. I pointed out that he would have been placed in the accelerated learning classes in Montana. Then she understood that he was bored. She was wonderful about doing anything she could to challenge him for the balance of the year. He was enrolled in the Idaho History class for accelerated students.

The next year seemed to be going along fine until his teacher kept holding him in class so he would miss the bus home. He would show up at the office and would have to sit in the break room for two hours. I confronted the teacher and demanded that she release the children so they would not miss the bus. The next day she embarrassed him in front of the whole class by telling all the students that Ray's mother had caused a scene. He was horrified. From that day forward, if I had an issue regarding his education I would have to discreetly talk to his teacher or simply not address it at all. It would bring him to tears to know that I was even going to try to get something straightened out.

She alone had demolished the trust that Ray and I had built up regarding school issues. He would no longer share his school problems with me, and if I wanted to get something figured out I would have to do it on my own. The teacher's final act of retaliation was to hold his report card without any cause. After all the other students had their report cards for a week, I showed up in her classroom and demanded the report card. She handed it to me without any comment. I was extremely disappointed by her unprofessional behavior.

CHAPTER THIRTY-SEVEN

Life went on without much fuss except for the loss of our oldest dog, Samson. He was now just over ten and began to have some serious internal health issues. It was something that surgery or medicine couldn't stop, so we lovingly cared for him until he finally gave us the look that told us he was done with life. We called the vet and he came to the house to administer Sam's eternal sleep.

For three nights following Sam's his death, Rich and I felt the bed suddenly shake, just as it had every night of Sam's life. He used to come into the room at bedtime and forcefully rub up against the foot of the bed before finding his favorite spot on the floor for the night. It was his way to say goodnight. It wasn't like just one of us felt it; we both did. How could this be happening when he wasn't living anymore?

This phenomenon led me to purchase my first book on life after death. I chose the book *Talking to Heaven* by James Van Praagh. James is an intuitive and psychic. My traditional faith upbringing certainly didn't provide any answers for me. Maybe I needed to check out what alternative thinkers had to say. I had seen an interview with Mr. Van Praagh on television and found what he said very intriguing. Was Samson trying to "talk" to us from the other side?

After reading the book I became much more curious about the beliefs of psychics. Too much of what I read made sense to me and it helped a great deal to discover that the author made it clear that faith in God is the foundation of his work. I had always been told that psychics only worked for Satan – they were not God-fearing people.

As for Sam's rubbing the foot of the bed? That was explained this way: If the mortal being (animal or human) died before it was supposed to, the spirit of the being could choose to remain on the earth realm until the time arrived that he should have died. That made perfect sense to me.

As owners of pets, we make the choice of what day and time we have the vet administer the drug that euthanizes the animal. I had been feeling so guilty about making the decision. I felt like I was committing murder and yet I could see that he was so close to death. I just could not watch him suffer anymore. He couldn't get up off the floor. He just lay there watching us freely move about, looking up at us with the "I would love to come over to you for a pat on the head or a rub-down" look. What I read meant that he decided to hang around for three more days. And bumping the bed was his message to us that he was freely going where he wanted to and that he was as happy as he could be. He obviously just wanted us to know he was happy.

I talked about the book with friends. I worried that some of them might think I was studying witchcraft. My insides told me I was finding the right answers and taking the first steps on the right path, but my conscious mind instilled fear of social rejection. People would think I was crazy. Oh well, if I got negative responses, I would just keep my beliefs to myself.

I pondered more and referred to the book when a small event would happen that affected me. Typically I found my answer there. I shared my thoughts with Rich and Ray. Neither of them thought I was crazy as they too were wondering about the same things.

Our other dog, Alf, did not know what to do without his dad around, and suddenly my house seemed eerily quiet, as the two were no longer competing for the alpha-dog position. No more would I have to explain to someone on the phone that I did not own a grizzly bear, it was just the two of them in the same room growling at each other.

CHAPTER THIRTY-EIGHT

The local recreation center provided many youth sports so Ray was able to play flag football and basketball. When he entered Middle School he no longer wished to participate, as the teams would now be chosen by "draft" and he just wanted to play for fun. He never wanted to prove that he was better than anyone else. This meant the end of athletics for him.

Ray excelled in math until he was required to show his work and memorize the steps required to get the answer. He could get the answer without any "steps." Me? I required all the steps plus tutoring to understand them and any mathematical concept beyond barebones math. Ray just understood it. He found information on the internet on how students in Japan or China learn math skills, proving his point that the US method was a waste of time and not the best way. Science was also a natural for him and he had a phenomenal memory. Any assignment that required memorization was no stress for him. He was so much like his father when it came to intellect. He refused to get straight As because he didn't want anybody to think he was better than they were, so he always made sure he had a couple Bs and maybe a C mixed in. It was frustrating for me to see him not doing his best. We were never very happy about the Cs, but he was happy and doing well, so we just asked him to do a little better.

Middle School for Ray was a time of experimenting. He tried skipping school, cigarettes, marijuana, girls, and being with a group of kids who were stealing from the local market. He was also old enough to take driver's education in eighth grade. What a huge step for mom and dad! Suddenly it was time to think about letting go . . . a little more.

He spent more time with friends after school and overnights, as most of them were old enough to be left home alone between the hours of three and six p.m. It helped that I knew several of the parents. He joined an afterschool medieval role-playing/gaming group that was organized by one of the schoolteachers. The students created and developed their characters, which included acquiring money, goods, weapons and food. It was interactive and required a great understanding of what one needed to live and survive in those times—or in any times! The students loved her for allowing their imaginations to come alive.

Ray had a wide variety of friends, from the straight-A students to those who were constantly failing. With no ethnic boundaries, he had established one friendship that ran deeper than a sibling. Brandon was his best friend, hands down. Rarely would they spend a day without being together. They could always be found at one home or the other.

The biggest event for our family was planning, saving and sending Ray off to the East Coast. The Math / Driver's Ed teacher put together a Heritage Tour trip each year open to eighth grade students. It seemed quite expensive, but we had heard nothing but rave reviews. We cut back everywhere we could to save money for him to go. We ate a lot of Ramen Noodles and pancake dinners to make it all work financially. It was stressful, but worth every penny saved.

My boss Jeff had a daughter who was one of Ray's classmates. She would be going on the trip and Jeff would be going as one of the chaperones. How ideal. Ray had an established relationship with Jeff, and Rich and I would know exactly who would be keeping tabs on him. Ray would truly have a fun time as he would not have to deal with the loneliness and anxiety that comes from being far away in a strange place. Ray's daily calls home were made that much better by getting a personal report from the chaperone, as they were indeed hanging out together. They both had a great time. My boss's daughter was more interested in being with her friends, so everything worked out well.

Ray had used all the rolls of film that he had packed, wishing he had taken more. He was able to experience the things he read about in textbooks. He had never seen a skyscraper, the Air and Space museum, Statue of Liberty or real Amish people in their own environment. He saw a Broadway play and professional basketball game, the White House, Jefferson Memorial and the theater where President Lincoln had been shot. He had never had so many people around him all the time. And yes, he visited the Twin Towers, all the way to the top observation deck—the same buildings that would be destroyed four years later, on September 11, 2001, from an act of terrorism.

He came home with little shot glasses from all his favorite places and a tie-dyed T shirt that he purchased from a street vendor. This shirt would become his identity. He wore the shirt every single day—for years. Yes, years. After so many weeks of wear and many washings each week, it developed weak spots that soon became holes, which eventually became huge gaping open areas. He always wore another shirt under it, no matter what the weather. It was hilarious how over time you would see more of the under-shirt than the tie-dyed shirt. When it finally was holding together by only small groups of threads, I hid the shirt so he would be forced to wear other clothes.

As Ray's level of learning progressed, so did the results of his work. His art projects became treasures. The pencil sketches, pastel paintings, free-form art and pottery pieces reflected his imagination and need for perfection.

Rich and I were just working, working, working. I would try to get home by six. Rich would get home whenever he could. Some days he would be home before five, but most days he would call me to say he needed to go have a "pop" with so-and-so to discuss an issue. That just meant we wouldn't be seeing him until dark or after, and we most likely would not be having much conversation with him that evening.

We purchased our first personal computer when Ray was four. Technology was changing and improving quickly, so we now upgraded to the latest and greatest model. Ray understood as much as Rich, so after a bit of research they requested all the components that would work best. They both spent a lot of time on the machine at home. If Rich was working on it, Ray would play his video games until it was his turn. Between the two of them, there was little time for me to use the computer. That was okay with me, because I wasn't fascinated with computer technology like they were. I enjoyed sewing and needle-crafts, so I was usually busy making something. We all had our hobbies.

We never felt like we had any extra money to spend on an exciting vacation, because we were making two mortgage payments every month (we had purchased the additional acreage) in addition to a car payment. We tried to go golfing and soaking at the hot springs resort a couple times a month to give ourselves a sense of reprieve from the daily grind.

Our vacations during those first five years of living in Idaho consisted of going back to Montana to see relatives. The first two years were enjoyable. Then we went because they all wanted to see us again. Then it dawned on us that none of them would bother taking their vacations to come and see us, yet they all demanded that we take our vacation time to see them. We were done with them dictating our lives.

Finally we began taking one week in the summer to travel to a place other than a relative's home. We went to Glacier National Park and the surrounding area, then ventured to the Oregon coast. When Ray was a sophomore we decided to go to Anaheim and San Diego to enjoy Disneyland and the San Diego Zoo. Ray was now in High School so the things that Rich and I wanted to see and experience were also things of interest to Ray.

Brandon went with us on the trips to Oregon and California. Having another person in the group made it that much more fun for all of us, and Ray had someone to goof around with.

High school had its ups and downs for Ray. At fifteen plus Ray was ready to enter the work force, as he had his sights set on a new guitar. We had purchased one for him a couple years earlier. He had learned to play and enjoyed jamming with his father. He was now ready for a high-quality instrument. He knew the only way he would get it was to earn the money himself.

Walmart had just opened a store in our community so he took it upon himself to apply. He was discouraged when he was told that he was a little too young. They could not hire him until his next birthday. Thank goodness it was only a couple of months away. He made his next application the day after he turned sixteen. He was given a schedule and began working part-time as a cart collector, putting in as many hours as he could during the summer months. He soon had enough money for his guitar and before we knew it he owned a beautiful new Fender Stratocaster. Rich and I complimented his new acquisition with a new professional amplifier for Christmas.

He terminated his employment with Walmart when a calling center opened. A neighbor friend was a manager there. As timing would have it, Ray had just gotten the spacers installed to prepare his mouth for braces. For several weeks the folks receiving his calls thought he was mentally disabled because his speech was so impaired. He found a lot of humor in it and did quite well taking advantage of the sympathy factor. However, soon work began to be much less satisfying, and it didn't take him long to discover that he absolutely hated being a salesman. He and the manager mutually agreed that he was not cut out for telemarketing. Ray was out of work.

He immediately got another calling center job. This one was a survey-based system, not sales. He didn't enjoy it but didn't want to give up the freedoms that came with earning a wage.

He had helped his dad with work at inventory time and now inquired about working there on a regular basis. Rich made sure that Ray understood that he didn't want to see him working the rest of his life at a truck dealership, but did encourage Ray to experience something other than Walmart and calling centers. An opening for a parts delivery person became available and Ray was hired. He was almost twenty, had a good driving record and had proven that he could be punctual no matter what the shift hours were, so his dad was confident that he would not be embarrassed by hiring his own son.

The work was only part-time to start with, but the pay was much better than any of his previous jobs. Within a few months he was promoted to full-time and enjoyed talking with the older men about "guy-stuff" like sports, weapons, machinery and technology.

Ray was always well-liked by his classmates and was voted a Homecoming King candidate his junior year. One of his friends won and he was perfectly okay with that. In his senior year, his classmates begged him to be their class president, but he refused to allow them to put him on the ballot.

Because he was not involved with athletics, he gradually gained weight. He now viewed himself as fat and decided to do something about it. He investigated and studied many diets and weight-reduction methods. We talked about those he found most interesting and weighed the pros and cons. He knew that he would get discouraged easily, so we chose the popular Adkins Diet, with a few adjustments. I allowed him to do it if he faithfully worked out and chose one day per week to eat and drink anything and everything he wanted.

The plan worked and he lost fifty pounds in about six months. He was feeling great and looking awesome.

As we all do when we decide to "diet," he started eating more of what he desired without thinking about the accumulated results. His weight started creeping back, bringing with it feelings of failure and low self-esteem.

During his senior year, he became so frustrated and down that I took a day off from work. He was so depressed that I didn't dare send him off to school in the morning. We spent the entire day talking. He was so lost. He had no goals. He didn't know who he was, what he was up to or where he was going. Most of his friends had developed a career path. They all seemed to have a solid direction. He felt there was something wrong with him. Our discussions included religious beliefs, social morals and mores, politics and education. He did not have any solid beliefs other than acknowledging a Supreme Being and denying the existence of the Devil. He viewed Satan as a human-created scare tactic by religious leaders. He also refused to be a conformist in our society. He grew his hair long and wore the same shirt every day— he would have done much more if his dad and I would have allowed it. He just didn't like to conform. He didn't know where he belonged.

After many, many hours of dissecting his life, thoughts and values, we decided that he needed to make a change in his life. He would not get out of this funk without making a change—any change. We talked about picking up a hobby like bicycling, golf or fishing, taking an art or pottery class at the college or finding another volunteer job that would give him some sense of value and accomplishment. I didn't feel like we had solved his problem, but we certainly got his wheels turning.

Within a week he declared that he was now a vegan, and he explained to us how he planned to stay healthy. He proved that he had researched this thoroughly, so from that day forward he never consumed meat or animal products. After talking, he and I decided he needed to make a change, but it never occurred to me that he would make such a dramatic one.

Rich and I could not make the change with him as we found great satisfaction in the flavor and textures of a good cut of meat. Ray would have to help me find ingredients and recipes and he understood that he would need to be more involved with cooking. He actually liked the idea of spending more time with me in the kitchen and making choices for himself at the grocery store. It was routine for him to go shopping with me and he already did a fair amount of cooking, so these aspects of his transition would be no big deal. He now had a goal and sense of direction and self-esteem again. It was all a good thing.

CHAPTER THIRTY-NINE

Graduation day arrived before we knew what happened. He looked so handsome in his cap and gown! I could see that he felt good all the way through. I could see it in his eyes.

Rich and I had not been able to go to college, so we strongly encouraged Ray to get a degree—any degree. He would be able to supplement a basic degree later in life much easier than trying to start from scratch when he might be married, have a family and a full time job. We assured him that we would do whatever we could to help him get through. We would pay his tuition as long as he did well, and he could live at home as long as he liked.

His biggest challenge was that he had no idea what he wanted to study. He was a natural with computers. Math was not a challenge, nor was anything science-based. He had attended the career classes and events in high school that were suppose to identify what each student was suited for. Even getting the ACT report and seeing what he excelled in didn't inspire him. Everything the tests identified were careers that he almost despised, such as being a banker or computer programmer. He just didn't know.

Many of his friends went off to be mechanical engineers or other highly technical studies. We all decided that it would be best for him to attend the community college ten miles away. That way he could get the feel for college life and see if he found something that would interest him. He could then transfer to a four-year college. This would also allow him to keep working.

He didn't have any trouble juggling work and college, although we soon saw his grades decline. There was nothing to blame but lack of interest. He got an A in his computer and science-related classes and failed or barely passed everything else. He was not enjoying college. By the first semester of his second year, we all agreed to stop the torture and allow him to quit college.

He honestly didn't know what he wanted to be when he grew up. This dilemma became more intense. He was not content with his life. He wasn't depressed, he just felt uneasy. He didn't understand why he couldn't figure out what excited him. All of his friends something they were passionate about. They all had dreams of being something. We had many, many conversations about it, but decided it would come in its own time, and we just needed to be okay with whatever life held for him at this time. There was a reason for everything.

He decided to build a computer of his own from the ground up, ordering every nut, bolt, wire, cord and card necessary. As usual, he thoroughly researched everything. His friends were amazed and jealous of his ability to build such a state-of-the-art machine. They called on him more now than ever to help them out with whatever problem they were having with their own computers. He would grumble about their ineptness, but would never consider NOT helping a friend.

From the time Ray was in high school he seemed to always be constructing something of significant technological value; adapting his Nintendo machines to run pirated software or adapting them to run on his state-of-the-art computer. He would go to yard sales to see if he could find old gaming systems. When he found an Intelevision system with a large number of game cartridges, he was so excited. When he researched the computing ability of the system, he didn't even try to play it; he had found himself an "antique" and he just wanted to say he owned one.

152

If we were having any trouble with our family PC, he would always have the "bug" fixed without any effort – some cursing, but no stress. Computers and their way of functioning were so elementary for him. I was always impressed. When I studied computer operating, the computer took up a whole room of the school and the disks were eighteen to twenty-four inches around. If you dropped the set of cards that you loaded to boot the whole system, you were in a world of hurt. Now the disks were down to three inch squares, CDs were now available and the internet was up and running on the screen in an instant. I guess it was good that we introduced him to the machines at such a young age; he knew no limitations and was always excited at the improvements that were right around the corner. He now talked of nanotechnology and entire computers being part of a person's body cell system.

He tried to build a homemade movie theater; using an old television, cardboard, black spray-paint, a special magnifying lens and high intensity light bulb. I never completely understood that either, but it didn't work nearly as well as he felt it should have.

After this, he decided to build an arcade game machine. He had a friend whose father owned or worked for an arcade, so it wasn't long before he purchased a broken unit. He gutted the entire box, designed his console, ordered the lights, switches, wires, buttons, roller-ball and all the other techno pieces he needed. He had over four thousand games downloaded from the internet, assembled everything and cursed like a sailor when his shooting system wouldn't work. Every other game worked except for anything requiring a "gun." When his friends would come over, he would try to pick their brains to see if per chance they would have the magic answer for him. No one did. They were just in awe of his abilities and wanted to play his machine. To heck with the gun! A good portion of the basement room was sacrificed to the movie theater and arcade game. There was no way I could take the vacuum to that area of the house as there were hundreds of tiny screws, springs, bits of plastic, metal and tools – tiny tools--discs and anti-static material everywhere.

If he needed a break from his project he would pick up his Fender Stratocaster and practice his favorite tunes. He was always trying to play as accurately and as fast as Dimebag Darrell of Pantera. He had learned a few Jimi Hendrix and Stevie Ray Vaughn tunes in addition to some improvised blues and hard, hard rock "melodies." Are there really any melodies in hard, hard rock?

As far as vehicles, he started his driving days with our old Chevy four wheel drive pickup; something we felt he would be "safe" in, although it had a hair-trigger gas pedal and fairly touchy brakes. Its name was "Old Blue" and Rich would always tell Ray to be careful because it was capable of climbing a tree. A Volkswagen Beetle was vehicle number two, when he decided he didn't like paying for the gas that "Old Blue" guzzled. Then he decided that he didn't like not having any heater and was tired of looking at the pavement through the floorboard, so we upgraded him to a Honda CRX. The small yellow car had a lot of character, and he absolutely loved it. It was small enough to get great gas mileage, but had a large enough interior to be very comfortable for himself, a passenger and both of their computers when they were off to a LAN party. He installed a high-quality stereo/sound system, including those huge speakers placed in a homemade low-profile "case" and made other small modifications to the interior.

Life was good for all of us now. Ray was busy working and enjoying a lot of time with his friends. He was refurbishing the Triumph TR6 and was almost done putting his Kawasaki Vulcan Classic motorcycle back together. Rich seemed content with his work and social time, and I was busy with work, Kiwanis, Beta Sigma Phi and my handmade creations.

We all seemed to be in fairly good health. Rich had had a heart problem during the summer of Ray's sophomore to junior year, but the stents did their job and his heart was working fine. He also had a hip that gave him a tremendous amount of pain. He put up with it for years. As the pain got worse he was forced to gradually reduce his golf games. It finally became so painful that he found it difficult to walk much or sit in the car very long. He no longer wanted to go on vacation as it would mean sitting in the car for too many hours. After Ray graduated we managed to get him to go to San Diego one more time—a graduation gift for Ray. He limped along in pain. Ray and I limped along behind him when he wasn't paying attention, mimicking his gait. Rich would have been so angry if he knew we were making fun of him.

CHAPTER FORTY

Fall arrived before we knew it. Alf had been our only dog for the past seven and a half years. He was now more than twelve years old, still very active and healthy, but he no longer jumped off the deck like he did when he was younger. One day in late September or early October, he came to me in a very different way. He nudged my leg with his nose, circled me, looked up, sat for less than a second and then repeated the behaviors. He had a "help-me" look in his eyes, but I had no idea what his problem was. Within a few hours he could no longer use his back legs. I called doctor Bob, the vet, who diagnosed a broken back and kept him overnight. He made phone calls to a veterinary college in Colorado to see what the latest successful treatments were. Injections of human spinal cord injury drugs were given. No improvement. Alf was not in pain, he just couldn't use his back legs. There was nothing more that Dr. Bob could do, so we brought him home.

We made a nice comfortable bed for him in the family room at ground level. He was so confused when he would get up and not be able to travel to the place he wanted to go. He was strong enough to pull himself around in a room but couldn't go up or down stairs if his life depended on it. He tried going down once and started to tumble. Thank goodness Ray caught him or he could have suffered even more injury. When he needed to go out to do his business, Ray and I would take turns holding his back end up. We found that using a bath towel like a sling under his belly worked well, but it still wasn't easy to walk behind him while at the same time holding up about forty pounds. We had to walk with our legs far apart so we could straddle him and keep our own center of gravity.

Ray and I did this for weeks. As each week went by Alf became weaker and ate less. He got to the point where he couldn't give us the signal when he needed to go out. He was so embarrassed when he would mess on the floor. It was so sad to see him this way. By the end of October he quit eating altogether. Finally, during the first week of November he gave me the look: the "I want to be done with this life look."

I made the call to Dr. Bob that none of us want to make and made the painful request for euthanasia. Bob knew how dedicated we were to our dogs and he was very compassionate in how he spoke to me. He again came to the house. With Ray and me by his side, Alf received the shot that would send him to dreamland forever. Then Bob left. Ray and I stayed on the floor with Alf, stroking him and telling him, "It's ok to go, big boy. You are a good dog," until he breathed his last breath.

I had a Beta Sigma Phi meeting that night that I could not miss, as I was President of the club that year, so I gathered my wits and left Ray alone to deal with Alf. Rich was home but not able to help Ray because of his hip.

When I got home, Ray's eyes were still watery and red from crying. While I was gone he had dug the hole and buried Alf along with his favorite blanket and toy. When I reached out to put my hand on Ray's shoulder in consolation, I noticed that he had cut his bangs. Ray had been sporting a popular hairstyle where the entire head was shaved with the exception of bangs....very, very long bangs. "Where is your hair? What did you do?"

All he could sputter was "For Alf." He had cut the hair and left it with the dog. Wow!

We now were family without a pet. The house felt empty. It took Ray and I several weeks to stop getting teary-eyed when we spoke of him. We all decided that we would go the winter without a dog as potty-training in the winter would not be any fun. We would re-visit the idea in the spring.

Without warning and to our surprise, Rich announced that he was going to get his hip fixed. He had made an appointment with the bone doctor to find out exactly what had to be done. Rich hated doctors, so Ray and I rejoiced that he was actually doing something about it. Surgery was scheduled for January 28th.

Ray came down with a nasty cold/flu virus right around Christmastime and continued to suffer with it all through January. I was amazed that Rich didn't catch it, as they were working together in addition to living in the same house.

Rich had the surgery. The doctor was amazed that he was able to add over an inch to the length of the affected leg. He had not seen a patient go through the pain of losing that much joint and bone before getting the hip replaced. The surgery went well. Ray purchased a bouquet of flowers and waited for his dad to come out of post-op.

Rich hated hospitals so much that he insisted on performing the necessary therapy exercises the second day after surgery. The doctor promised him that if he could do what the physical therapist demanded he would be discharged to go home.

The therapist was a "Nazi Drill Sergeant," as Rich put it. He despised her. He went up and down the stairs, nearly passing out getting it done, just so he wouldn't have to deal with her another time. As promised, he was discharged. Home therapy was set up. I took a couple days off work to help him get around when the therapist wasn't visiting.

The doctor put him on powerful pain medication that made him hallucinate, so as quickly as possible Rich discontinued it. Because of Rich's past drug use, I was always worried that he would take advantage of the prescriptions and become a prescription drug addict. Within three weeks, I could see that my worries had no merit.

CHAPTER FORTY-ONE

On February 27, just before ten p.m. we all decided to go to bed. Rich still did not have much range of motion with his hip and was using a cane. The two sets of stairs up to the bedroom took him a while and took a bit out of him. It was Sunday night and we all needed to get a good night's sleep for work the next day.

Ray was in his room seated in front of his computer, as he usually was when he was in his room. Rich said goodnight to Ray while I shut off all the lights. I then went up to the bedroom, making the ritual stop by Ray's room to say, "Goodnight." When I saw him on the computer I added "Don't stay up too long. You need a good night's sleep. I know how excited you are about getting your motorcycle parts, so try not to stay up too long."

Rich and I climbed into bed, turned off the lights and began to doze off.

All of a sudden I heard a big clang; what I thought was my big roasting pan hitting the counter—like it had been dropped. This startled both Rich and I from our feeling of euphoria, that floating feeling you get right before going to sleep. I immediately rose to one elbow, looked at Rich, and we both said, "What the hell was that!?"

I got out of bed and headed to Ray's room first to see if he was there. I hadn't heard a door shut, so I was certain that he was still in the house, although I thought that I had heard him go down the stairs.

"Ray?"— no reply… he wasn't in his room. I then went to the landing of the stairs that led down to the kitchen and then to the family room. Before I went down the stairs I paused and called for Ray again . . . "Ray?" Still no reply.

Again I called for Ray as I continued into the kitchen. Just as I rounded the corner of the wall into the kitchen I could see his ankles and feet on the floor. Oh my God!! Why is he on the floor?

Two more steps told me everything. There he was lying up against the cupboards, eyes closed like he was sleeping, except that there was a small pool of blood under his head and a hole in his right temple.

The scream that I let out included every speck and molecule of being. "NO!!!! NO!!!" RAY!!!!"

I quickly surveyed the kitchen, seeing a handgun on the floor along with other bits of something. Rich was at the top of the stairs before I knew it, his face ashen with incomprehension and disbelief. He hobbled down the stairs as if he had no restrictions and was kneeling at Ray's side in a heartbeat. We both felt him for a pulse . . . yes, there was a pulse. I could also see it in his neck.

I grabbed the phone and called 911. I was shaking so bad that it didn't go through the first time. I quickly dialed again. I blurted out our address and that our son had just shot himself and the ambulance needed to get here as fast as possible. I knew it would take ten minutes, but also knew that we may not have that much time.

Rich stayed with Ray while I ran up and down the stairs. In and out of the house I went; all the while on the phone with the 911 dispatcher. All I could say was "HURRY!! HURRY!" "THEY'RE NOT HERE YET! I CAN'T SEE ANY LIGHTS! WHERE ARE THEY? THEY NEED TO HURRY!"

Rich kept asking me if I could see them yet or if they were here. I would run down the stairs and run back with my report. Quickly I figured out that our truck was in the way, so I grabbed the keys and moved it, running, shaking, screaming at the dispatcher.

My boss was a volunteer fireman and had moved into a neighborhood one mile away only a few weeks earlier, so I requested that the dispatcher call him to get him here. I also asked if they could call an Idaho State Police officer that I knew lived a mile in the other direction. The dispatcher said they were contacting Jeff, but would not be contacting the ISP officer.

Somehow I thought that if one of them could get here before the ambulance and EMTs that they could save Ray.

As the minutes ticked by the pool of blood got larger. Ray's body was turning white and his hands were turning blue.

Oh my God, my son!!! Not my son!!! Not RAY!!!

I have no idea how long it took any of them to arrive, but I do know that they indeed were "quick responders." My boss, Jeff was one of those to arrive early. He brought his girlfriend with him.

We told the first responder through the door that we had not touched anything – not a thing. Then we got out of their way so they could tend to Ray. Many different providers showed up. The house seemed filled with men in suits; some with badges and guns, others with patches with medical symbols. They all were there to do anything they could to help Ray. One of them was a chaplain; the only female among them.

It didn't take long for the chaplain to tell us that he was gone. Jeff and his girlfriend were sitting with us when the statement was delivered. The shock of what we were going through was so intense that we were numb. My mind felt like a small box that someone had crammed tight and overflowing with a bunch of vibrating bugs. The vibration emanated throughout my entire body.

I didn't want to go home after Patrick died. This time I didn't want to leave.

My hearing became acute beyond anything I had ever experienced. I could hear a pen on paper in the other room. I could hear the people breathing. Every sound they were making seemed loud to me. I felt like someone was dissolving my guts. My head and body hurt from the vibration and my insides felt like they were leaving me. I felt sick to my stomach and I was shaking. I would get hot and stuffy so I would go out onto the porch in the cold February night until I could breathe more easily, then back in to sit with Rich, then to the bathroom. I felt like throwing up, but never did, however my body evacuated all contents through other orifices.

Ray had never been baptized, as I always believed he could make the faith choice on his own when he was ready. Now was my last chance to have my baby baptized. The chaplain went into the kitchen and came back to tell me that she could not baptize him. I don't believe she gave me a reason, but I didn't question her. If I did, I didn't hear her reply. To this day I do not know why she could not.

I led Rich, Jeff and his girlfriend in a prayer to take Ray into the loving arms of the Lord and give us all the strength that we would need at this moment and beyond to make it through this tragedy.

Questions came from the Sheriff's detective: "Was he depressed? Did he ever threaten suicide? Was there anything that we could think of that would have led to this act?"

No, no and NO!! We told him that he was very happy and excited for the next day as he was expecting motorcycle parts to finish his bike so he could ride again.

Rich said, "He was on his computer. Go see what he was watching!"

The detective went to Ray's room, coming back to report that he had been watching "Reservoir Dogs" and looking at tattoos. Nothing there.

As active members of our community, I was friends with the mortician. David arrived and gave me a deep, caring hug, promising to take the very best care of Ray. I knew he would. There was some comfort in knowing who would be watching over him until we made the decisions that were now before us.

The sun began to rise and light began to come into the room where we had been sitting in the dark. A new day that only delivered pain. We were both so numb. We managed a few words between us. "I don't know how we'll make it through this." And "What the HELL was he doing with a gun in the kitchen?" Neither of us could answer that question.

We made the heartbreaking phone calls to our siblings and my father, telling them of our tragedy.

CHAPTER FORTY-TWO

Sometime that morning three or four of Ray's friends came to see us. One of their mothers had driven them as none of them were in any shape to be driving. They were so very devastated. They were all such close friends. They spent so much time together playing computer games, always having so much fun. They gave each other emotional support in every way. Their hearts were broken.

They stood there sniffling and crying, asking what happened. When we told them everything we could, we stated that we didn't have a clue why he had a loaded handgun with him. Their body language changed in a micro-second! Their mouths came open and their eyes widened. "You don't know?" one of them finally asked.

"Know WHAT!?" we demanded.

"We can't believe he never told you." "He always carried a loaded gun with him if you were in bed or gone."

"WHY?"

"Well, ever since Alf died he's done that."

Ray was not comfortable without his dog and he NEVER said a word. The information was of great assistance to us as we were so confused. Why did he shoot himself when he was so excited? Now we knew – or at least we thought -- it was NOT on purpose.

Independent, tough Ray would never let on to his parents that he was insecure about anything, especially the security of what a dog brings to the family. However, we were so grateful that he shared his feelings with his friends.

They stayed for a short time, offered assistance in any way possible and left.

Before the friends had gone, the detective returned, asking if he could do some measurements as part of his investigation. We encouraged him to do whatever it took to get the answers we were all in need of. Soon there were two or three more law enforcement officers in our home. After spending a fair amount of time in the kitchen he came down to visit with us. They had found where the slug had gone and needed our permission to cut a hole in the ceiling to retrieve it. At this point neither of us cared what they did to that area of the house.

I know we received more visitors and neighbors but that is still a blur. Everyone asked if there was anything they could do. The only thing we wanted was yesterday, the only thing we wanted was Ray, alive and well as he had been the day before. When they offered food, I politely declined; explaining that in the past 24 to 48 hours Rich and I combined had only been able to eat four small squares of saltine crackers and a glass of water. Maybe in a few days our systems will be ready for food again. Quite honestly, neither of us cared if we ever ate again. Dying would have been just fine. We knew, however, that Ray would not agree with this behavior, plus we needed to do right by him and at least give his friends a chance to say goodbye.

At about thirty-six hours post trauma, I gathered the strength to go into the kitchen. It looked quite normal, except for the gaping hole in the ceiling. As I grabbed the handle to the refrigerator to get something I noticed the microwave flashing. Curious; I opened it to find a flour tortilla with cheese on a plate. I ran to the stairs. "He was fixing himself something to eat!!!!" All I could do was cry, "He was fixing something to eat! It was not suicide!"

Again I could barely stand. What little life I had drained from me again. I remember calling my brother and not even introducing myself. All I said in sobbing pain was, "He was fixing himself something to eat. He didn't do it on purpose."

The next day the detective came back again to see how we were doing and to let us know that his findings indicated that it would have been impossible for Ray to have purposefully pulled the trigger. The angle of the shot was done with the hand so awkwardly turned that it just couldn't have happened with intent. We reminded him that the safety on that certain pistol could be released without notice and the trigger had no resistance to it at all. From the day they purchased it, Rich had hounded Ray about how easy it would be to make a mistake with that firearm. Rich and Ray were fanatics about firearm safety. Ray would return from target practice with friends and state that he would not be going out with them again because of their carelessness, and that they probably would not be asking him to join them as he was all over them about it.

Ray's friends came to visit often and wanted to be part of making the arrangements, so I gave them the task of music and allowed them to help pick out his shirt. It was their decision to have a viewing, and the service was planned to accommodate their schedules. After the viewing, but before the service, Ray would be cremated, just as he wanted.

The mortician was so pleasant to work with. How they can make such a traumatic event a calm, orderly and meaningful occasion is truly a gift from God. He even thought to have the orthodontist call to see if we wanted his braces removed. No, he was proud of his braces, he was so glad to be able to whistle. He adored his orthodontist and would sometimes stop at his office just to say "Hi."

None of us had been attending church, so we chose a pastor who was a member of one of my service clubs. Ray absolutely loved his art teacher from high school, so we asked that he present Ray's life sketch. He was honored and had a few stories to tell of his own. In his preparation, he viewed the artwork that we displayed in the house. He asked if he could take two of them and frame them for us. We didn't see them again until the viewing. The framing brought out the detail of the works. As for the service music and place—the only place large enough was the LDS stake center and Ray's kind of music would not be allowed there, so we asked a young lady who had graduated from high school with him to sing. I asked that she choose the song as she had known Ray well. Her mother, who I knew through the service club, would be playing the piano.

The viewing was difficult and the service even more so. I asked a friend to sit beside me, and she had to wrench my hand off of hers during the services I was squeezing it so hard.

There were so many people at his service that some had to stand. What an honor to have raised a son that so many people knew, liked and cared about so much. There were people 16 to 85 years old, there were people with tattoos and piercings and folks who normally wore suits and ties. He crossed all lines in his friendships—really, there were no lines. His friends came from all ethnic and economic backgrounds.

There would be no internment as Rich and I needed to make a decision on where we would keep Ray's urn, and that of Ray's little brother. Until then, we would keep Ray's ashes at home with Patrick's.

CHAPTER FORTY-THREE

I just sort of floated through my spiritual and emotional life until Ray's death. I didn't buy any other books or read much of anything. My energy went into creating through crafts and needlework. I gave away almost everything I made as gifts.

Ray's death shook my world in a way that basically recreated me. I felt like I was just a shell . . . nothing more. I was completely empty inside.

As Rich and I sat in the dark the night Ray died, we suddenly heard strange noises at the entry door on the other side of the room. This was considered the back door. We always used this door or the one in the garage because there were no stairs and they were nearest to where we parked our vehicles. It was such a big racket of thumps and screeching noises. It was definitely not a person. When I opened the door and peered through the storm door I could see that it was a bird! A raven, to be exact. The bird was screeching and pecking at the door. He was trying to use the outside light as a perch, leaning over to the door so he could peck at it; his wings flapping like crazy against the siding and the door as he screeched.

We had lived in that home for twelve years and in all those years never once did a bird try to get in – especially at that door. There was nothing inviting to a bird there. Robins and barn swallows nested under the eaves of the patio roof every year and once in a while one would fly into a window, but the door had only a small window in the top center; a good eighteen inches from where the bird was flapping.

Rich and I looked at each other..."What the heck is that all about? What does that bird think he's trying to do? And why?" We had no explanation. I just couldn't shake the sense that the bird was trying to tell us something; like it was screaming at us.

Two or three days after Ray died we prepared to go to the mortuary for the first time. Rich went out to the truck as I grabbed my purse and a quick sip of water. As I stepped outside and closed the garage entry door behind me, I noticed he was looking up and pointing. He wasn't pointing so I could see, he was pointing like he was reaching upward. As soon as he noticed me he said, "Did you see that? You should have seen it. It was the biggest, blackest bird I've ever seen! It was bigger than any raven or golden eagle in Montana. You remember how big they can get? It was bigger than that. It was huge! And it swooped down over my head and called out. I've never heard a bird make that sound before. I could even hear its wings. I don't have a clue what kind of bird it was." He was in awe.

I did not get to witness the event. The bird was there for Rich and Rich only. As we drove to the funeral home he said, "I think the bird the other night and this one was Ray. How could we have two totally weird bird things happen so close together? Ray loved black. Both birds were black."

"I don't understand it, but what other explanation could there be?" I said.

Somehow both birds' strange behavior brought us a speck of peace. It was so unusual that we had to believe that it came from the spirit world.

CHAPTER FORTY-FOUR

Within a couple days I forced myself to use the kitchen and begin cooking again. As I opened one of the lower cupboards I found a small chunk of hair and scalp that the cleaner had missed. I handled it like a delicate butterfly. Through my tears I placed it in a small Ziploc bag and had yet another breakdown. I couldn't share my discovery with Rich as I feared that he would become very angry. He was in enough pain, physically and mentally; I didn't need to make it worse.

I knew without speaking about it that Rich was feeling guilty about letting Ray own firearms. He was with Ray each time he purchased one.

Ray began showing interest quite early in life, as almost every drawing he did included some sort of weapon. I always passed it off as a "guy thing." Rich and Ray always talked high-tech in their discussions; guns were just a part of those talks. By the time he was in his mid-teens his goal was to own a firearm as soon as he turned eighteen. He met that goal, and from that time on he and Rich were always gun shopping. It was good father/son time.

After serving his time in Vietnam, Rich had vowed to never own a gun. He had many friends who hunted and were always trying to change his mind. He stood firm--until Ray could not be dissuaded.

Me? I had learned to fire a gun as a youth, took the firearms safety class and occasionally joined my brother gopher hunting. For me it was target practice and I never ever hit a thing. I didn't have a strong opinion about guns until Ray was born. All of a sudden I didn't want them around. Rich had purchased a toy gun for Ray when he was about two and a half and I hid it high in the cupboards. It was safely out of reach until Rich found it and gave it to Ray like a new-found treasure.

Rich knew how I felt about them, but also knew that denying Ray the right to own a gun when he was of legal age would not work. The best he could do was advise and educate Ray on firearms, so he could make wise choices for ownership. He also took him target practicing so he could teach him how to properly handle a loaded gun. He did all he could to make it as safe as possible.

Ray had many rifles and handguns. He and Rich would ask me what I thought each time they talked about buying a firearm, knowing that I would strongly object. It became a game with them to see how upset they could make me. I would give them every reason I could think of: people die from their own handguns protecting themselves more often than an assailant's gun – so don't tell me it's for protection. They are too dangerous, they are too expensive, you don't need ANOTHER gun. I could never win, but I could certainly object.

The handgun that fired that night was the only piece in Ray's collection that Rich was concerned about. The safety could be released silently, with little to no effort. When the detective let us know that he would have to take the gun, we gladly let it go.

So now, here we were, facing the unthinkable. How could we lose our loving, caring, conscientious, loyal, happy son? What did we do to deserve this? How could we lose BOTH of our children? We dedicated our lives to Patrick...Did we NOT pay our dues? How could the Lord take them both? How could he take our happiness away? Ray WAS our happiness.

We were SO happy together . . . we were like the Three Musketeers. If Ray and I weren't talking, he and Rich were. If he wasn't with his friends he was with us. He and I cooked together, shopped together and did inside and outside house fix-up projects together. He would stay outside with me when I was gardening just so we could talk. As a family we went to movies, soaking at the hot springs, out to eat, pleasure drives, we did everything together. He was an adult and always knew his time was his own but he chose to spend it with us. He could move out any time he liked. He always said he didn't mind living at home and planned on staying until we sold the big house— if that was ok with us.

Rich and I had been planning our retirement, which was scheduled to occur two years down the road. The year before Ray's death we had purchased eight acres of property in central Idaho and planned to build our retirement home there. Yes, Ray helped choose that lot. Rich would continue to work for his company as a management consultant, mostly from home, so that we could have health insurance and a small income. We were in the beginning stages of preparing this home for sale.

We suffered greatly every day. I could not manage to go back to work for two weeks. Once I did I tried very hard to do the job that I was being paid to perform, but it was so difficult. I would break down in tears at the drop of a hat. I would close my office door and just slump into a corner with the box of Kleenex. Most often the co-workers would let me be, but sometimes they would come in to help console me. Sometimes I would just run into Jeff's office and say "I have to leave for awhile." I would take a drive or walk to the Catholic Church that had a nice peaceful place to sit outside.

CHAPTER FORTY-FIVE

On Wednesday, three days post trauma, we sat numb and motionless, watching television like zombies, then Sylvia Browne came on. Blindly staring at the TV came to an end. We listened intently. So much was contrary to everything I had ever been taught about spiritualism. I did not understand everything she was saying, but she had piqued my interest.

Now I had to begin reading again. I wanted to learn more about crossing over. I purchased one book written by Sylvia Browne and read it in record time for me (three or four days).

Her theory that we create a contract with God and other spiritual entities for our mortal life, choosing the challenges that we want to experience while on earth was sounding plausible. But why on earth (excuse the pun) would I have chosen to have children only to lose them? Was I an idiot? Did I think I was superwoman or something?

The information about being totally able to communicate with people who have died seemed an unattainable goal for me. She was saying that we all have the ability, we just don't use it. We grow up being told that our imaginary friends are not real, that there's no way we can communicate with anyone on the other side and that we are weird or possessed if we think we can. We are pretty much programmed not to talk about the things that the older humans have decided are impossible. We are shut down as soon as we are old enough to express our thoughts. We are indoctrinated in the beliefs of our family.

Reading all this uncovered an ember of life and hope in my empty soul, which was like a void inside, fragile, like I could crumble into nothingness at any second. I cried and cried and prayed and prayed. I hurt in a way that is so difficult to express. My heart hurt, my brain hurt, and the pain emanated from those central spots to every cell of my body. The pain made me feel weak, like I had nothing left in me. The sadness was so dark and ran so deep that there was a numbness about it. My body would sweat for no apparent reason, or I would become cold or hot. I had no desire to feed my body. I didn't care if I lived. Dying would be welcome. What was there to live for? My baby, my son, my friend, my only pride and joy had died. What was left for me here? I was sure there was nothing, until I read Sylvia's first book.

If I had truly entered into a contract, a sacred contract with God, what was my purpose here? I did not die with him so I guess it is not my time, I guess my contract is not up yet. Hmmm . . . And when I had him I made the choice to stay . . . hmmm. I'm supposed to be here for something. For what, I don't know, but here I am, still breathing . . . damn it.

I made it a point to talk to faith leaders of different denominations to see if any of them could share some wisdom and give me a flame of hope. Maybe if I started going to church I would find my answers. After I got back to work I was able to visit with a Monk from the priory, bishops from the LDS church, the Lutheran Minister, a non-denominational pastor and the pastor of another church in town. They all shrugged their shoulders and explained that God gives us things and takes them away. It is not for us to know why. He is the Father, He knows what is best for us and should He decide that punishment is in order He will deliver. There it was again. Punishment! If I was to be punished why couldn't it be me and my body? Make me a quadriplegic or take away my sight and hearing! But to take away my children? God would never do that as

178

punishment! And what the hell did I ever do to deserve punishment? This was NOT punishment!

God loves all his children. God is good. God is kind. God is Love. These faith leaders were more confused than I was. These "leaders" were simply other humans. After picking their brains I got nothing worth keeping. To my surprise, those of the LDS faith I spoke to were the least judgmental and the most open-minded. Yes, they had their specific beliefs, but they listened to me more and contemplated what I asked and shared of my thoughts. Again, I had been reared to believe that of most all other faiths practiced in the intermountain west, LDS was the worst.

Through my work I had had frequent contact with members of that faith and occasionally was asked to consider joining their church. I found some of their practices very unique, but I found that I had no business "judging" them for what they believed. Now, in my time of need, I found great respect for them as individuals.

What I found after talking to them all was that each faith had strict boundaries around what they believed. There was little or no room to wonder, or wander – no flexibility. Everything is "this is the way it is." Period.

I pondered. If so many faiths believe that if you aren't one of them you are going to hell, what about all those generations, thousands of years of generations before their faith was ever established? Did all those people really go to hell? Come on! So many of the faiths practiced today were established because someone decided they didn't agree with what they were taught. What right do they have to create walls? The originators broke free of the walls placed around them. It just didn't make sense to me.

I have always believed that we are all individuals and we each need something different to make us feel warm and safe in our faith. That said, I cannot criticize any faith on its fortress of teachings because we

179

need all different belief systems for different comfort zones. As long as the faith does not worship Satan and encourage deviant behavior, I say let them be. Encourage them to thrive. For me? I just can't endorse walls of any sort. Many of us need walls to help us feel safe or boundaries to give us the sense of knowing what is right and wrong. Find the walls that you can reside within. Give thanks, give love, be kind, be gracious and be safe.

As the days and weeks went by, I continued to struggle with my lifelong faith and what I was reading and learning. I wanted to integrate them together, but the feeling of guilt remained. Was I headed in the right direction or was I just so grief-ridden that I was grasping at anything, real or not, that made sense at the moment?

The thought of going through five years of crying and depression and another five years to get myself together again was not welcome. That was my pattern of grief after Patrick's death. I worried that if it was a total of ten years for Patrick, when I had two and half years to prepare; what was it going to be this time when it was so sudden and there had been zero preparation time? The future looked like a long, long, dark journey.

The independent warrior in me rose up and expressed, "We know this battle! We've done this before! Let's get on with it and get it over with! Charge!!" I wanted to get through each phase of the grief, check it off my list and be done with it! Then the realist inside would say, "Oh, Sandra. Things take time. Take your time. Let it happen in it's own time." AARG!! I was angry that I had to go through all of this again.

I hate pain, I despise depression. I'll just stay busy as soon as I have some strength.

I went back to work where I could be distracted most of the day. It helped, but it did not keep the sadness and pain away. Sometimes it would actually make the pain and depression worse because I would be tired. One night's sleep could not replenish the precious energy I had spent. That would mean several days of physical and emotional weakness, which, in turn, made for more crying and hiding in the corner of my office.

CHAPTER FORTY-SIX

Thirty days after passing Ray came to me in a dream. It had taken Patrick seven months to show himself to me in dreamland. One month! I was so pleased!

The dream was very vivid: Ray and I were at a small community picnic. The day was beautiful with the sun shining so brightly and birds singing in the background. The park was very large, the grass looked vivid green and smelled wonderful. The area where we were enjoying the company of friends was loosely enclosed with a white picket fence that only partially surrounded the place. It was there for beauty, not restriction. Some friends were standing around while others were seated at picnic tables. Everyone was smiling, talking and acknowledging each others' presence. Ray and I were standing just outside the fenced area. He was at my right side. In the left corner of the fenced area there was a three-sided cardboard box – no top. Inside the box were two German shepherd puppies sitting up, side by side, shoulder to shoulder. They appeared to be around twelve to fourteen weeks old. They were still cute, but they were past the fuzzy-haired roly-poly stage. They were content sitting in their corner, happy to be at the picnic and their ears stood straight up listening to all the friendly noises. Their eyes sparkled and their faces almost looked like they were smiling.

Ray and I were deciding which one we wanted. "What should we name her?" I asked Ray. He gave me a name, but I couldn't register in my brain what he said. I said "I'll never remember that! How about Anna?" As I asked, I turned to look at him. He was smiling at me with a "That's a good name, that will work just fine" look.

Suddenly we were in a new location. I was outside of a cedar-fenced yard. Ray and Anna were on the inside. Suddenly Anna came through a panel of the fence that magically created a doorway. Down the fence and around the corner she went. There was a big trampoline in the backyard. Ray bounced off that and over the fence with no effort. Off he ran after her. I couldn't tell if they were playing a game or not. She was sporting a bright red collar. Attached to the collar was a matching long leash.

Dreams are always strange in that they begin, change scenery and end without notice. Almost always, no matter how strange the situation or grotesque things or people are, the dream seems real. It's only when we wake up and start analyzing what we just experienced that we then label and question.

Ray paid me a visit! We were happy together! We were making a decision together, just like we did when he was alive! With excitement I had not experienced in many weeks I conveyed my dream to Rich. I felt energized! There was a smile on my face that I wasn't forcing. There was a smile on the inside, in my heart. It was as if I had received a wonderful letter or loving phone call from him, there was such a feeling of connectedness.

I cried because I was happy, then because I was sad. I could not ask Ray about why he ran after the puppy. He wasn't here. He was only in my dream.

I gathered my wits and made my way to work. Even though I had realized his true-life absence, I still felt joyful. As soon as I got to work I shared my dream with my co-workers and Jeff. They embraced the dream as a gift from Ray. I had the very first good day at work. By evening, the darkness, emptiness and weakness returned. Ray's visit was only a vision in my mind. It wasn't real. He wasn't real. Just a dream . . . that's all. Just a dream.

Rich and I talked about getting a puppy. Before Ray had died we talked about it, but had not decided on the breed. Did we want a small dog or a large one again? We didn't know what we wanted.

After the dream and with what I had been reading about the spirit world we figured we had better start looking for a German shepherd. Neither of us had much strength, but it gave us something to do with our time away from work.

It wasn't too many days later that we were watching a program on television about a search-and-rescue team. The handler was running after her dog in search of a lost child. Rich and I quickly turned to look at one another when we saw the red collar and matching long leash and the trainer calling the dog by name, "Anna."

Our eyes opened wide like we had seen a ghost. Rich said, "Your dream!"

I turned away to look at the TV. As he said those words I was seeing "Ray Moore Road" on a street sign. I urgently said "Look! Look! Did you see that?"

"See what? I was looking at you!"

"The sign. The street sign said "Ray Moore Road!!" I was struggling to get the words out fast enough. We just looked at each other again in amazement. How could this be? How could I have a dream and then see so much of this on the TV?

CHAPTER FORTY-SEVEN

I purchased another Sylvia Browne book and had been reading other books provided by a friend who embraced psychics and life after death. Had I not been accepting at some level that spirits do indeed communicate, I probably would have thought I was going crazy and seeing things that weren't there. I was definitely intrigued by what I read.

Meditation was a huge part of Sylvia's work. She didn't give enough information in her books for me to learn to meditate, so Rich bought me a book. It began with very basic, short meditations. If I found it beneficial, I could progress to more detailed and more focused sessions. As I began to practice I found that I gained a tiny, tiny amount of peace. Kind of like when you are looking at a five thousand piece puzzle strewn all over the table and you find two pieces that fit together. It doesn't seem to matter, but you know it's the first step to putting all those pieces together again.

Recovering from losing Ray has been the biggest challenge of my entire life. I lost my entire sense of being, my entire reason for living, all joy in daily life. I had my soul sucked out of me. I think I will be working on getting all if it back for some time yet.

Friends would ask, "How are you managing to keep yourself together? I don't know how you are doing it."

"How do you get through your day? I couldn't live if I lost one of my kids. I just can't imagine what you are going through."

My inside voice would reply, "I'm not together, I don't KNOW how I'm doing it, and I agree—I would rather die, I would rather not live,

I wish I were dead. What do you mean ONE of your kids!!! Try ALL of them!!"

Verbally, I would say, "I don't know how I'm doing it. All I can do is look down at my feet. They only go one direction. I can't go backwards so I guess I have to go forward. One foot in front of the other. And don't even try to imagine what it's like. I don't want you to go there. It's not easy. The only way I can eat this elephant is one bite at a time. It's going to take me awhile."

Customers I had been dealing with the past twelve years had a difficult time separating work from friendship and love. A real estate question that should have taken five minutes turned into a one-hour talk. I could sense their awkwardness.

The company I worked for treated me as an injured child; caring, nurturing and loving me with everything they could offer. The president of the company came several times to check on me. I'll never forget him calling me into the conference room where he had been meeting with Jeff. He looked at me and asked "How are you doing?"

Through my tears I said "I have never hurt this bad in my entire life!"

I did not look him in the eye when I made my statement. When I lifted my glance I saw that he was crying. He cared so much. He assured me that he and the other managers and employees would do all they could to help me through this painful time.

So, here I was again, going through the loss of a child. I not only lost a son; I lost my only child; I lost my identity – again! This time my identity as a mother—my whole purpose in life. Losing Ray meant that I would never, ever be a mother again. I would never have a child to speak to or speak about with others. I would never see my child married, or see him happy with his own children. I would never ever be a grandmother. The thing I loved most about my life was being a mother. My heart, soul, and purpose in life had been ripped from me and torn to pieces. I felt like life had just sent me through a paper shredder. There was nothing left of me but a pile of bits and pieces. How could I ever, EVER become whole again?

CHAPTER FORTY-EIGHT

I could not touch Ray's room. Things were left exactly as they were that night. I would open the door to his room and just sit there crying. I could smell him there…it was the last bit of him that we had. I just couldn't let that go. I wanted to hear his voice and touch his skin. I wanted to see that little glint in his eyes when he spoke to me that said, "I love you." My life had been shattered and I wasn't finding any solace.

Mother's Day came on May 8th: A very, very painful reminder of what I had been just three months before but WASN'T on this day—or any other coming day! How wicked that our nation would have a day to recognize mothers! Nothing like driving a stake into what little essence of heart I had left! What about those mothers who were mothers, but would never be again?

On the morning of May 14th, at about 9:15 a.m., I received a call that my mother had just died while eating breakfast with other residents of the nursing home. It was her 69th birthday.

It had only been ten weeks since Ray's passing. Oh, my! Not AGAIN!!!

My mother had been suffering from dementia for the past twelve to fifteen years. My brothers and I knew "Mom was losing it" a couple of years before I moved to Idaho. We were all hoping that the forgetfulness and repeating would subside or go away on its own. To our disappointment, it only got worse.

My father did his best to care for her while still working full-time at the sawmill. He had always been very "laid-back." I don't remember him demanding anything. He could have been content living in a dirt cave eating only bread and water. Consequently, cleanliness was not important to him.

My younger brother had never moved from our hometown, so he and his wife got very involved in Mother's care. They were finally able to convince Dad to take her to a neurologic specialist in the city when she no longer knew what a fork or spoon were. The diagnosis was "galloping dementia." The prognosis was that for as many years that we could remember seeing symptoms, there would be that many years left to her life. After a lot of reflection we estimated that she would probably live another seven years or so. The doctor would have her consigned to a nursing home as soon my father was ready to take that huge step.

As her disease progressed, my little brother and his wife helped more and more. They tried to arrange some in-home care, but the house was in such poor and unhealthy condition that no one would continue working for them. Most of them threatened to call adult services. Finally mother began to break the mirrors in the house and leave dirty bathroom tissue everywhere. She had now become a danger to herself and my father.

With much pain and reluctance, my father finally admitted her into a nursing home in the city when she was sixty-one and my father just sixty-six.

I just wasn't emotionally ready to handle another death so soon after Ray. To make things worse, two years earlier my family decided that I was to be the executor and conservator of her estate. I was the only child who lived out of state. My father and younger brother still lived in my hometown and my older brother lived in the city where mother now received her care. Nonetheless, I was the chosen one.

Appointing me conservator was not such an issue, but the family divisions culminating from the required legal appointment and filings were gut-wrenching. We had always been a family that got along famously—now there was a Grand Canyon between me, my younger brother and his wife, and an uncomfortable air between me and my older brother. Somehow I had become the bad guy. I could not, and still to this day, cannot understand exactly where it originated or the depth of the seething venom that came from my little brother and his wife. I did what was legally required and requested of me. I honestly do not know what I could have done wrong.

Reluctantly, I communicated with them in order to find out what was expected of me for mother's arrangements.

Dad had already chosen the church and pastor and I wrote her obituary many years earlier. Her funeral expenses had been pre-paid so that Medicare and Social Security would pay all the nursing home care. That money came from her social security income that had been collecting in her bank account while she was still at home. At least those items had been handled. I was given the name and phone number of the funeral home and pastor. I made as many phone calls as I could prior to leaving Idaho. Rich and I drove the five hundred miles the day before the service.

Mother had been cremated according to her wishes. There would be no viewing.

When I arrived at the funeral home to go over the details with the mortician, it was discovered that no urn had been purchased and no funds were available for one. I had nothing with me that could be used for that purpose and there was no time to order one. What was I to do? The funeral director was kind enough to let us borrow one for the service, knowing full well that it would be taken more than fifty miles away. I was given instructions on how to remove the box that contained mother's ashes and given a specific place to leave the empty urn when I returned to the city as they would not be open to accommodate my schedule.

Mother's service was simple. Most of those attending had been in singing groups with her. She had always loved singing and had been blessed with a beautiful soprano voice.

My family wanted me to sit in the front row with the rest of the family, but I simply refused. There was only one family attending that knew who I was, and I could not muster the strength to sit in the front row again. Not so soon after the last time.

As soon as the service was over my younger brother approached me asking, "When am I going to get my money?"

There was force in his voice, as if he expected me to give him an answer he would object to. I was taken by surprise. Why would he ask for money when he knew full well that the State of Montana mandated that she be penniless to be on Medicare? I asked, "What money? There IS no money."

He replied very sternly, red-faced: "You need to get me the money! Any money that is left is MINE! That was MY social security number on the account at the funeral home!!"

I could not believe what I was hearing. There was no money for her obituary to be printed in the paper, no money for flowers, no money for an urn. I paid for the newspaper expense and bought the only bouquet of flowers that appeared at the service. What was he talking about? I replied to him; "I saw all the papers that the funeral home had. Your number was NOT on them. AND I will NOT go to jail so that you can have money!!" "Would you like me to tell the Pastor that I cannot pay him for his services?"

"NO!!" and he stormed away.

What the hell just happened?! I exited the church as quickly as possible and took some deep breaths. I was still so emotionally fragile. This verbal attack in the house of the Lord took me by surprise. I had no time for anyone with a negative attitude. As I reviewed his statements in my mind I became so angry!

Rich had seen me leave the building and thought that I had gone out for something. When I didn't immediately return he came looking for me. He could instantly see that I was upset and asked me if I was ok; hugging me. "What happened?" As soon as I conveyed the conversation to him, he became enraged.

We had carpooled with my older brother, his wife and three children. Rich went in to tell my older brother that we were leaving. He asked which of his family members would be riding with us. I went in to grab the urn. Two of the children came out and climbed into our car.

As I was getting in the car, my father appeared asking why I was leaving. "I thought we might be able to visit."

Fighting back tears I said, "I'm sorry Dad. Things have changed. I have to go right now!"

Now he was crying. All he wanted was a little one-on-one time with his only daughter. I could not give that to him. I had no energy for the grief I was getting and I didn't want to discuss it with him. He had to live in the same town with my brother and his wife and needed their assistance and support.

Rich and I had indeed planned on spending some time there before going back to the city, but now all we wanted to do was to get back to Idaho. Because it was late in the day, we spent the night in a hotel in the city. We invited my older brother and his family to join us for dinner in our room and we had gotten it approved for them to enjoy the pools and hot tubs with us. We had a pleasant evening. As soon as we woke at 5:00 a.m., we packed and got back on the road. As we drove down the road we both counted down the miles remaining that would take us into Idaho – HOME.

After this last encounter neither of us wanted to have anything to do with the State of Montana.

Mother's passing was something that we knew would come, as she had been in a vegetative state for the past four years. I really didn't feel any grief or sadness. She had always had a deep faith in God and never talked of fearing her end days. The last time I visited her at the nursing home when she could still use her voice, she was singing. Wearing headphones to listen to her music on cassette tape, she sang along to her favorite songs. It was very eerie to hear sounds like an Indian ritual rather than the beautiful tunes I was so accustomed to hearing from her. I knew that from that day forward she was always singing in her mind. She had finally gone to the most peaceful place we mortals can contemplate. I felt peace.

I had just been through three deaths, each ten weeks apart; the dog, Ray and Mother. There's an old adage: "Three time's a charm," right? So I felt confident that the group of three was it. I was done with death.

Now it was time to work at getting my life together and moving forward.

CHAPTER FORTY-NINE

I got back to work as soon as we returned home from Montana and continued to read many, many books. In January/February I was in the middle of making a quilt for a friend. Ray had purchased fabric for a quilt that he would create with me when I completed the one I was working on. Now the sewing machine sat idle. All supplies remained as they were in February. I could not bring myself to sew. I cried just thinking about it. Ray had always been my sounding board and art critic. He would always help me arrange the pieces or pick out the right buttons or accent thread. Now I had no one to share my ideas with; no one to be proud with. Rich's standard statement was always; "I don't need to look at it. Whatever you make is always beautiful." The words were very kind and supportive, but he had no interest in the project...he usually didn't even look at what I was asking him about. He too was an artist, but somehow he never wanted to venture into this type of creation.

My creativity had left, so I spent my time reading. It felt odd to be so obsessed with reading when I had only read a small handful of books. Throughout my entire life I managed to read only a handful of books in addition to the four paperbacks in high school— just enough to pass a class. I had never before enjoyed or desired to read. Now I couldn't read enough.

Friends and their love and caring had much to do with my recovery. Even with so many who truly cared about me, I tried to end it all on Father's Day following his death.

Rich came to me to say, "I'm going to get beer. I'll be back." Normally I would have accepted that I would not be conversing with him for the balance of the day and I would do whatever, pretty much ignoring him until he passed out. I would go to bed and that would be that. I knew that this Father's Day would be really hard for him to get through, but I didn't expect him to give into alcohol. Since his hip surgery, he hadn't been drinking. I had been able to talk to him about my feelings and thoughts. I immediately felt abandoned and betrayed. He didn't even care enough to ask me if I wanted anything or if I wanted to go with him. I was already struggling that day myself. If he no longer cared about me and wanted to leave me, maybe I'm the one who should go. I had no tolerance for alcohol. A single mixed drink or one-third cup of wine could get me drunk. He has almost a full bottle of Vodka in the cupboard. If I drank all of it, I bet I could die. My body couldn't handle it.

I went to the cupboard, poured myself a ten ounce glass of Vodka, tossed in about an ounce of orange juice and drank about half of it without a hesitation. I took the glass to Ray's room and sat on the floor. I managed to finish the drink. The room was spinning and my head felt like it was attached to my shoulders with a wet noodle. I was already sad and crying. The alcohol deepened the sadness and made the pain worse.

I was disappointed that I was still conscious when I heard Rich return. He must have heard me sniffle or something because before I knew it he was standing in the doorway. "Are you ok?"

I was smashed–totally intoxicated. I tried to turn to answer him, holding myself up so I wouldn't fall over. "I don't want to live any more. I want to be with Ray." I slurred as I cried. Rich responded with, "Do you want to do this?! I don't want to be here anymore either! If you want to do it, I'll go get a gun and we can do it together! Is that what you want?!"

He was angry. He was shocked. I had never before used alcohol to soothe pain. I rarely had a drink of any kind. I just looked back at him. Finally I said, "No. I just don't want to hurt like this anymore. I can't do it anymore. I can't be strong anymore." He looked at me with pain in his eyes. He would have expected this on Mother's Day. This was his day to be acknowledged and here I was adding to his pain. He did or said something to console me and then left the room.

It was obviously not my time to go because even with all the Vodka in me I never passed out. I felt terrible for five days. I had done nothing but make myself more miserable, mentally and physically. Rich and I never spoke of it again. It certainly wasn't the smartest thing I've ever done, but I have never felt embarrassed about it.

Thinking about suicide has got to be very, very common and almost expected when someone loses one that's so loved, but following through with it is a whole different issue.

You'll go to hell if you commit suicide! I used to be quite sure of that. Not so anymore. After everything I had been through, I was thinking more that earth WAS hell and if you did yourself in you just had to come back and start all over. That would be hell enough for me! Who needs to go anywhere else to receive inconceivable pain and suffering? I had enough right here as a mortal being.

But what about the soul contract? The pain in my soul made me question more about how we end up with the lives we lead. What about my contract with God? Still, the contract theory made more sense to me than anything. And yes, one of the other things I had read about was that those who terminate their lives early by their own choice (not mental illness) do have to come back and finish out their contract. Hmm . . . do I believe that? Not sure.

CHAPTER FIFTY

As the season changed from spring to summer my passion for gardening also went missing. I managed to keep the existing perennial flowers and raspberries alive, but I did no new planting.

We began planning more seriously for our retirement. We purchased a used pop-up trailer so we would no longer have to pay for a hotel room when we went to work on our property. There was plenty of fallen timber to collect and burn and we needed to decide exactly where we would build our retirement home.

The Fourth of July was just around the corner, and we didn't feel like staying home. The year before Ray had set up his amplifier on the deck and played Jimmy Hendrix's version of the Star Spangled Banner for the entire neighborhood. Whistles and hoots came from every direction immediately following his last note. We just couldn't do the Fourth at home.

The weather was lovely in Central Idaho and the private campground a comfortable place to spend our evenings. We stayed for several days. On the morning of Ray's birthday, while in the process of cooking up breakfast, the metal lid from the little gas stove flew on my left hand. The gash in my index finger exposed a speck of bone. I went into the trailer, grabbed some water and our first aid kit, went back out, flushed it and laid the skin back where it belonged. Rich was dumbfounded. He kept asking me if I needed to go to the hospital. I told him I was fine and that it really didn't hurt that much. He helped bandage the wound and I finished breakfast. I too was amazed that I really wasn't feeling much pain.

Summer turned into fall. Rich and I were still simply putting one foot in front of the other trying as hard as we could to imitate a normal life. Our new puppy that I first saw in my dream was born on July 30th. We began driving an hour and a half once a week to spend time with her when she was just eight days old. We brought Anna home on September 30th and soon after began traveling to Sun Valley and other locations for the mandatory obedience training.

Ray's buddies came to see her. During the summer we had sold Ray's car to one of his closest friends. He was making payments to us and we were fortunate to be able to see him and some of the others nearly every month. It was always wonderful to see them.

The pain of not having Ray stung as each holiday came. Thanksgiving meant nothing to us. We purposely treated it as any other day. We would not be cooking a turkey with the fixings or making room in the oven for Ray's To-furkey. We wanted to be thankful for our many blessings, but right now we couldn't find anything to be thankful for.

Getting through Thanksgiving just signified that Christmas and New Year's was right around the corner. These weeks of the year were particularly difficult. Again, we refused to acknowledge the holidays. Our lives as parents had been destroyed. There was no joy to be found in the season.

Ray had always stayed up with us on New Year's Eve. He had only missed celebrating the coming of a new year once with us, but even then he called just before midnight in celebration. This New Year's only meant that we had survived the past ten months and that the coming year couldn't possibly be as bad as the last.

During the month of January a couple of my friends each visited with me about going to a counselor. Each of them referred me to the same person and each offered to take me to her. My friends were confirming what I already knew. I needed help.

CHAPTER FIFTY-ONE

I suffered eleven months of pain and emptiness. Bringing Anna the puppy into our home brought us distraction and simple joy, but it was definitely not her "job" to fix us. I wanted to find the magic wand that would make everything better again. I hadn't found anything yet.

Finally I started seeing the grief counselor. The first session was intense. She put me through a very basic meditation. "I want you to close your eyes." I tried to shut them and keep them closed, but my eyelids fluttered like a trapped butterfly desperately trying to escape. "That's okay. Just relax as much as you can. ... Now take a deep breath in." I inhaled only to discover that it was very difficult to take in much air. My lungs were almost mimicking my eyelids and my chest hurt. "Again. One more deep breath. Breathe into your heart. One more time. Breathe into your heart. Now tell me what you feel."

Oh my gosh! It hurt so bad!! It was like I was trying to fit an entire room's worth of air into a tiny bubble. This was how we started every counseling session. Each time I was able to report different heart responses.

As we talked and she gathered information about me, she drew on a large pad of paper on an easel. She acknowledged that I had suffered an extensive amount of loss in a very short period of time, much more than any other patient she had ever seen. She opened my eyes to the fact that "losses" did not just mean death. Loss included my childhood; I did not have one, the loss of my relationship with my younger brother; I had been his "mother" and now the entire relationship was gone, and it included the fragile relationships with my father and older brother. At that time they had both taken my younger brother's side of the issue. None of them were speaking to me. It was as if I was an orphan. "We can work on these things. Things WILL get better."

My counselor had a heart. She spoke softly and gently, yet had an air of authority about her. She shed tears as I spoke. She felt some of my pain. At long last I found a counselor I could talk to and who I had confidence in. If anyone could help me at all it would be this wonderful gift from God. I hugged her as I left the session and from the depths of my heart I said, "Thank you!"

The drive back to the office was an experience of its own. I could see myself driving! It was as if I was seated just behind my right shoulder, watching everything I was doing. I truly felt like two separate beings.

When I got back, I called her to ask about it. "Oh dear! I forgot to ground you again when we were done. Are you sitting down with your feet on the floor?"

"Yes" I replied.

"Stick your arms out in front of you and cross them. Then bring them into your chest, under and up."

I put the phone down, followed her instructions and then picked the phone up again.

"Did your arms fold against your chest?"

"Yes."

"Ok, good. When you hang up I want you to do that again. Then take a deep breath, exhale, release your arms and lean over and touch the floor. You should be fine after you do that."

Lo and behold, I no longer felt like two people.

After I had seen my counselor a few times we talked more about my inner beliefs and she referred me to a meditation/intuition teacher in Boise. It didn't take me long to make my first appointment with her and enroll in formal meditation classes. The combination of grief counseling and meditation gave me a lot of comfort and kept me moving forward in my journey.

CHAPTER FIFTY-TWO

In late March, Rich had his first business trip away from home. Because I had been seeing the counselor, Rich was finally comfortable leaving me home alone with Anna for a week. He wasn't feeling well when he returned home, cursing the sick passenger that he had to sit next to on the airplane for sharing his unknown illness. As the days passed he continued to feel worse. I encouraged him to go to the doctor but he always replied that he would get better if he could just get more rest. He would try going to work each day only to return home after a couple of hours. He had never felt this poorly for so long before. We knew that our immune systems were not back to normal, but also knew it was rather odd that this bug just kept getting worse. Within a week or so, Rich was having trouble catching his breath if he went up or down the stairs. Finally he gave in and got in to see his doctor.

The day of the appointment, April 12th, he called me at work to make sure I knew that he was actually on his way to see her. A couple of hours later he called again asking me to come home. This request was completely out of character for him. I asked him "Are you ok?" He cursed the nurses for making him walk to x-ray and continued with, "I'm exhausted. I can hardly stand up. Please come home."

I immediately went into my boss's office to let him know that I had to leave for the rest of the afternoon. Once home, I could see that he indeed did not feel well. I asked, "How did things go? What does she think is wrong?"

He said, "She wasn't sure, but she will be calling as soon as the results of the blood tests are available."

At about 5:40 the phone rang. It was the doctor and she did not demand to speak to him. She said, "We got the blood test results and there is a major problem. It could be cancer. I need you to bring him to the hospital as quickly as possible."

Oh my God! She just said the "C" word and she's talking about my husband! She had also given me specifics regarding white and red blood cells. I repeated everything to Rich. He grumbled but put up no resistance about going to the hospital. Again, I found his actions strange, but was so pleased that I would not have to be fighting and pleading with him to go.

We needed to get a few things together and I had to deal with Anna. She would have to go with us. I didn't know what else to do with her. It took us about an hour to get everything together. I got him to the hospital and he was admitted. They were prepared for him, so the process went smoothly. As the nurses were getting him into his bed and taking basic vitals, the doctor appeared. Her first words: "What took you so long? I expected you just a few minutes after my call!"

She was very kind about her statements, but again I found the behavior odd. Then it became clear; she began explaining to us that the problem with the blood was Leukemia and his numbers indicated an acute case. She wasn't sure exactly what she needed to do for him, but getting into the hospital was step one. She was waiting for an oncology specialist to return her call. As soon as she heard, she would give us more information.

Well, here we were—nothing to do but wait for her to return. Neither of us spoke. We just waited, keeping any thoughts in our heads to ourselves. She had given us enough of a glimmer of hope that it might NOT be cancer that we simply waited.

It wasn't long before she returned to tell us that she was sending Rich to the much larger hospital in the city ten miles to the south. She would allow me to drive him rather than go to the expense of an ambulance. She indicated that the oncologist on call would meet us there.

We went through the discharge process and drove to the other hospital. By now it was approximately 8:00 p.m. As directed, we entered the emergency room, giving Rich's name, his doctor's name and the doctor she was referring him to. They said they were expecting us, so again, the admissions process went quickly.

After waiting in one of the emergency patient "rooms" for a short time the head nurse came to tell me I was wanted on the phone. "My name is Dr. Blancher. You are the wife of Rich, correct?"

"Yes I am," I replied.

"Rich's doctor asked that I see him tonight but I am not at the hospital and there is no one else in the hospital who can see him tonight. I think we should probably have him admitted for the night where the staff can monitor him. They could give him some blood and I could see him tomorrow morning."

My only question was, "Do we have any other options?"

"The only other thing I can suggest is to take him to St. Luke's Hospital in Boise. Would you feel more comfortable doing that? Depending on what I determine tomorrow, there would be a good chance that I would have him sent there anyway."

That was all I needed to hear. "I will take him to Boise now." She told me that she would make sure that all the paperwork would be ready when we got there so he could be taken directly to a room.

We said our goodbyes to the nurses and off we went to Boise. We arrived at St. Luke's at about midnight. As promised, all admission documentation had been taken care of and he was whisked off to a room on the fourth floor in a wheelchair. As we walked briskly down the hall approaching the wing where his room was waiting, I looked up to read "Oncology Ward." This could be serious.

The third set of nurses that evening were busy getting Rich settled in. They made light talk about what we had been through to get there and that they would do everything they could to make his stay comfortable. When they inquired about where I would be staying I disclosed that I had no time to make plans. They told us that there was a room on the floor for family and that even though I had the dog with me they would try to get me into that room. It would take them a bit of time as it was in the middle of the night.

Nothing would be happening with Rich until around six or seven a.m. when the doctor would be making his rounds. Rich was exhausted and needed a bit of rest, so I went out to the car to let the dog do her business and try to get a little rest myself. I went in twice during the night, just to check on Rich. I got no sleep. I was too worried.

CHAPTER FIFTY-THREE

Early in the morning the doctor came in to introduce himself and do his basic exam. Blood was drawn and he said he would return to talk to us about the results the minute they were available. It wasn't long before he returned. The news he had for us was not what we wanted to hear.

Rich definitely had leukemia and it was acute. Rich was just barely healthy enough to try chemotherapy, but that could not start until after he received several units of blood. "So what would happen if we do nothing?" Rich asked.

"You could live up to two weeks, but no more." The doctor gave additional information on the process the body would take as it failed; basically that with no oxygen in the blood the entire body suffocates, destroying all internal tissue: he would bleed to death internally. If we did nothing that process would begin within the next few days. "Would you like a bit of time to discuss this and make a decision?" he asked with much respect and compassion.

"Yes, thank you. It shouldn't take us too long." Rich replied.

Rich and I had made a pact with one another that if either of us contracted a terminal illness that neither of us would treat it. Both of us still felt that we would be happier dead and with Ray than here on earth. We actually talked about that on our way to Boise. Now here we were; needing to make that exact decision. Suddenly our confidence about resigning to death was gone.

"What do you want to do?" I asked Rich. "I don't understand why, but I have the strong feeling that I am supposed to do the treatment.

I'm really ok with going. You know that. I think God is telling me to at least do the first round of chemo. I don't know why! Are you ok with that?"

It was uncanny that I too was feeling the message to try treatment. "I can't explain it either, but I am getting the same feeling. I guess we aren't supposed to give up so easily right now. You know that I would support you no matter what decision you made."

We just hugged for a while, sharing words of love and promised we would get through this no matter the outcome. No matter what happened, we would rely on those crazy messages. Finally I asked, "Are you ready for me to get the doctor?"

"Sure. Let's do this."

The doctor seemed relieved that Rich wanted to at least try treatment. He ordered more tests and started Rich on some drugs to get his body as strong as possible. The new blood he had been getting was breathing new life into him. Finally he was no longer feeling out of breath and exhausted. We were able to make the necessary phone calls to our employers, filling them in on what we knew so far.

We didn't expect to see the doctor until the next morning. That evening, however, we received a visit from him. He explained that the additional test had shown that the form of leukemia was so rare that there were no statistics in the United States and very few statistics from other nations. This leukemia had only been found in one-twentieth of one percent of patients with myelogenous leukemia. He had consulted with other leukemia specialists and would be trying a fairly standard chemo treatment to begin with. The treatment would take several weeks. He would need to stay in the hospital for the entire course because of possible infections and other side effects.

Oh, boy! Just when I thought I might be on the road to getting on with life, another huge challenge.

212

I had moved the car to the underground parking, so Anna would not get too warm from the sun. I went out to spend time with her every hour. I called my friend who lived in Boise. Without hesitation she opened her home to me. She lived about fifteen to twenty minutes from the hospital and made sure I had a house key so I could come and go as I needed.

We spent the first few days getting our affairs in order; talking about our current and future finances, what he wanted me to do with the money once he was gone and who we wanted to bequeath assets to in our wills. I called my attorney and scheduled an appointment. He would have the drafts ready for review as soon as I returned home. Rich also requested that I help him contact the VA to arrange for medical care. Rich had always cursed the American government and the department of Veterans Affairs for their lack of involvement, treatment and assistance for the men and women who fought for this fine country. In the past I had seen him become so angry about these issues that the last thing I would ever hear him say was "I want to talk to the VA." Surprise! He made the necessary calls and then I went out to meet the VA representative and bring back all the paperwork necessary to declare himself a disabled veteran. The representative was very responsive and managed to somehow get Rich approved for hospital care the same day we made the request. He had told me that the standard wait for approval was two to four weeks, so when he called us to tell us the news, he too was amazed with pleasure.

After a few days, Rich was stable enough that I was able to go back home, check in with work and get things together for the unknown. Again, Jeff and the other managers offered to do whatever it took to help me through this. I was granted the time off that I needed. It was very awkward for me to ask for more time off, but I had no alternative. I would quit my job if it made it too difficult for the company. I worried that I might be asked to resign and yet somehow knew that would not happen. The managers and employees of the

213

company were my family. Again a member of their family had suffered an injury. It was me–again!!!

I spent the next several weeks traveling back and forth to Boise. I found a day-care/boarding facility for Anna that worked with me on my unusual schedule and circumstances for the days that I would be away.

Anna had developed a serious health problem after being spayed. Her pancreas stopped working completely. She would scarf down everything we gave her to eat like it had been days since her last morsel. Everything seemed to give her diarrhea leading to many more trips outside than normal. It took a long time to figure out what the problem was and by the time we did she had lost a lot of weight. She was finally diagnosed and began medication shortly before Rich had gone on his business trip. Poor thing looked like skin and bones. The pet-boarding place was very accommodating when it came to her special feedings, medications and "bathroom" requirements. I would take Anna out for walks along the nearby river at least once every day. Our time together was precious to both of us. The sounds and smells from the water and all other nature elements provided great therapy.

By the middle of May, Rich was released to go home. Ten days later we went back to Boise to see if the chemo treatment had worked.

The blood results were not good. The treatment had taken a bit out of him but he still felt much better than he had in early April. The test showed that the bad blood cell count was actually higher than when he was first diagnosed. It was almost like the disease was an army that had been attacked, regrouped and returned with more troops. The leukemia had gotten stronger! The doctor suggested another round of chemo, this time the recipe would be more potent. Without much discussion we agreed to another round.

Rich had suffered some of the side effects during the first course, but the doctor thought he had done well enough that he suggested that

214

Rich rent a room in a house that the hospital had available for patients and their families. The house was only one block from the hospital so if he began having complications he could be back in the hospital within minutes.

Rich lived in that house throughout the entire second course of chemotherapy. I continued traveling back and forth and working part-time.

Again he was discharged to come home. This time he was able to stay for approximately three to four weeks because the doctor in Boise arranged for Rich to have blood tests and blood infusions at the hospital ten miles from our home.

He again returned to work while we waited for his blood cells to do their thing. His company and employees had called him daily to review an issue or solve a problem. They valued every moment that he was able to be at his desk or by their side. They too had become a family and his family members wanted their "big brother" back home. They all looked up to him with great respect.

The end of July was near and it was time for Rich to see the Boise doctor again.

We could sense the doctor's uneasiness as soon as we laid eyes on him. We braced ourselves for the news. "It doesn't look like we'll be getting good news today," Rich said to me as we followed the nurse to the little room where we would wait for the doctor to join us.

"Hello again. How are you doing? How are you feeling?" the doctor started.

"Not too bad...could be worse. What do the tests tell us?" Rich replied.

"As you know, the form of leukemia you have is extremely rare. We have tried everything possible and I have no other treatment that I can give you. Your blood tests show the counts are even higher than before we started the second course of chemo."

"So, the leukemia doesn't like the chemo and is almost feeding off the treatment," Rich interjected.

"I guess that's one way of looking at it. The chemo has just not been effective. I have nothing left to offer. I'm sorry."

We had gained a lot of respect for him over the past few months and completely trusted him. We could feel his helplessness, frustration and sense of failure. We thanked him for everything he had done and tried to do. We talked about what to expect during the anticipated surrender to the disease. The conversation was quite matter-of-fact. Rich and I were beyond showing emotion. We drove home without talking very much.

CHAPTER FIFTY-FOUR

One or two days later, Rich received a call from the doctor. He had contacted one of his oncology mentors who practiced and conducted research at the Huntsman Cancer Center in Salt Lake City, Utah. He was wondering if Rich would consider going there to participate in a medical trial run by his mentor. He would make the necessary arrangements if Rich was interested.

Rich quickly asked me what I thought. I was impressed that the doctor had continued to try to find additional treatment! I just asked Rich "Are YOU interested? This is YOUR body. What do you want to do?"

Without much hesitation he told the doctor that he would like to participate in a trial. If it might help the medical community find a treatment for this form of cancer, he could end this life in a giving way.

The doctor made an appointment for Rich to see the research oncologist in Utah and gave us the phone numbers we needed. Within a week we were on our way to Salt Lake City and found ourselves sitting in front of this doctor who was considered to be one of the top ten oncology specialists in the nation. This appointment was very intensive; blood tests, a more than complete physical and many, many questions that needed to be answered. This appointment took the better part of the day, and the specialist agreed to take Rich on as a new patient.

Rich was admitted that day. Staff came from another part of the building and escorted us up to his new room on the fourth floor. The building was gorgeous. The glass front let in lots of natural light, the hallways were wide and the colors comforting. His room was huge compared to any other he had occupied at the other hospitals. It was set up like a welcoming apartment; with the exception of the hospital bed and all the tubes, equipment and monitors along the wall nearest the bed. The windows looked out onto the huge multi-level patio where patients and family could go out and enjoy the beautiful weather and fresh air.

The hospital's policy was to allow a spouse and one pet to live in the room with the patient. "Even a German shepherd?" I asked.

"As long as the dog is friendly, we have no problem with any breed of cat or dog," was the reply.

I had housed Anna at a boarding facility forty-five miles east of our home because it was on the way to Salt Lake City, and I had been dealing with the owner for the past eight months, purchasing the special brand of food for Anna that I could only get in Boise or Sun Valley or from her. She was very friendly and caring—her entire business was clean and friendly.

I stayed with Rich a few nights while the specialist conducted even more tests to determine if Rich would be an ideal candidate for the clinical trial. There was much material to read and many waivers to be signed if he qualified. The side effects could be quite severe, including, but not limited to entire areas of skin blistering and falling off, permanent organ damage and even death. The more Rich read about the trial, the more he wanted to participate. If the new drugs could cure future leukemia victims he wanted to be part of it.

In the end it was determined that Rich's leukemia was too acute and the body/cell damage from the previous chemotherapy courses eliminated him as a candidate. He was quite depressed about the elimination. The specialist was, however, very intrigued by Rich's form of leukemia and asked if he would consider one more round of chemo; this time with a very special "recipe" that he had recently developed with fairly good results. The drugs would present a few more side effects than those experienced so far. He would also get Rich onto a bone-marrow transplant waiting list. Hopefully a match would be found soon.

This chemo was not part of the trial, but was still a bit experimental with no promise of cure, so Rich did not hesitate to undergo more treatment.

Knowing that he would be staying for at least six weeks, I arranged to get home to put the things together that we would be needing. It was comforting to both Rich and I that Anna would be "living" with us. We could be a family right there in the hospital.

My dear friends of Beta Sigma Phi offered to help me with anything, including driving me back and forth to Salt Lake if I needed it. I took them up on their offer and three of them drove down to pick me up as I did not feel safe traveling the four plus hours alone.

A friend from work insisted on driving me back to Salt Lake as soon as I was ready to "move" into our new little hospital apartment. I was a little emotionally fried. My friends recognized that and their kindness will be appreciated to the end of my days.

When I visited with Jeff, filling him in on our latest medical challenges, I told him all the details and said, "I don't know if Rich will be coming home with me this time. I might end up coming home alone. This is our last-ditch effort and it may not work."

"Keep us posted and let us know what we can do for you."

I thought that Anna might be happier spending the majority of her time at a boarding facility where she could be around other dogs, but she became very destructive during her first forty-eight hours. I could see that the chemistry between her and the employees of the kennel was not good, so I brought her to the hospital. Anna's health issues remained prominent and putting her in a stressful hospital setting didn't help much, but she was much happier with us than away from us. I did end up finding another boarding facility, so I could get her out of the hospital for spells. Sometimes I would let her spend the night, other times she would spend a good portion of the day there so she could play with other dogs.

I was back to getting no sleep. Like Patrick needing attention every hour, Anna needed to go out to do her business every forty to sixty minutes, around the clock. Nurses and doctors were in and out of the room so often that it really didn't matter. We were still trying to figure out the right enzyme medication dosage and food soaking time. Her poor little body had been so deprived of nutrition. To make things worse, I had taken her to a vet the day before coming to Salt Lake because she had started to walk funny. X-rays showed hip dysplasia. There was nothing that could be done for her now. Once my life settled down again I could visit with the vet about what to do about it.

I became friends with two other wives and a mother of an eighteen year old while I was there. The eighteen year old had the same form of leukemia as Rich. We all helped support each other. Anna was also fine support for others. Every time we passed the teen's room she wanted to see him. Nurses would come into our room to ask if Anna could visit a patient in another room. She was always happy to see them until it was time for them to die. Three times while we were there she would not enter a room when called. The first time it happened, I really didn't know why she wouldn't go in. I made my apologies to the family for her behavior. Three hours later we were told that the patient had died. The other two times I also made apologies for her knowing full well what was happening.

The first couple of weeks ticked by. The chemotherapy was indeed more difficult but he made it through the course of treatment. We waited the two weeks for the blood counts to improve. Then, as part

220

of this new program, a bone marrow biopsy was taken. The procedure was very painful for Rich and the results took longer to get. Two days later we found out that the leukemia still thrived in his blood.

The specialist was disappointed but gave us hope if he wanted to go through some more. Rich agreed to yet another round with an even stronger "recipe." Because the specialist was not using conventional drug combinations, the length of time that Rich had be to on the "recipe" was just one week vs. three. The waiting time to watch the blood counts remained the same at about two to three weeks. Just a couple days into the chemo, Rich began having much more serious side-effects. He was very weak, had hallucinations, his oxygen levels went way down and had many infections that did not respond quickly to the antibiotics. It wasn't any fun for either of us. We counted down the days until the drugs would be discontinued, hoping that this was the magic recipe. Then we waited for the blood counts. During that time Rich and I talked about what he wanted to do if this round failed.

As the days went by, the blood counts moved in the wrong direction. Our conversations got more serious. The bone marrow procedure was ordered and the specialist offered to try again. We could see that he was frustrated. The researcher in him wanted to conquer this rare form of leukemia. He wanted to win and send his patient home to live his life. Rich told him we would think about it for the day.

He had been staring at the ceiling contemplating when I broke the silence to ask "Do you want to go through more hallucinations, pain and infections?"

He turned to look at me, "You know, I think I need to be done with this. Nothing is working. Every time I go through this the counts get worse. This shit is killing me and the drugs aren't even touching it! I just want to go home. I just want to go home and spend whatever time I have left doing what I want to do."

"That's ok, if that's what you want. I'm just really jealous that you get to go be with Ray before me," I said. Without saying the word "die" we both knew *exactly* what going home meant.

Then he continued, "Before we tell them we are going home, I want the results of the bone marrow test. You KNOW they can get the results to us quicker than two days! We need them today— not sometime tomorrow or the next day. If the results aren't magically better, I'm gonna have to "*Chu Hoi*.' Tomorrow is Friday and I want to go home tomorrow." *Chu Hoi* was a term he learned in Vietnam and used frequently; it meant to give up, to be done. He no longer felt strong and had lost a lot of weight. He was so tired of feeling sick from all the drugs.

I said, "I will go make sure they know we need the results NOW."

I left the room to find the nurse. Once I located her I told her we HAD to have the test results NOW. She looked at me curiously because we had always been so easygoing about everything. Suddenly I was demanding something, and she could sense my certainty and determination. "Is there a reason you need them right now? I think we were expecting them tomorrow afternoon."

"We have made a decision and need the results right now! We can't wait until tomorrow. Please request them now."

"Ok, I'll get them as quickly as possible. I'll see what I can do."

From that moment on I would ask each nurse who came into the room if she or he had the results. I think every nurse on the floor knew of our demand. It wasn't long before the doctor on the floor came in to see if they could calm our urgency. Nope, it was a futile effort. Late that night, the doctor returned with the information. It wasn't what we wanted, but it was what we expected. The leukemia count was very high. It was odd, but we felt more relief than disappointment. Rich said to the doctor, "Thank you so much for pulling whatever strings it took to get the numbers. I won't be doing another round of chemo."

Early in the morning, as with every morning, the entourage of medical students arrived with the doctor on duty. We had gotten to know many of them, so conversation was rarely strictly medical talk. The cheerful greetings took place followed by the required patient review for the students. At the end of the review, the students were allowed to ask the patient questions. I don't have a clue what the question was, but Rich quickly responded with, "I'm done. I want to go home. I want to be released TODAY."

The room became totally silent. The entire group of medical professionals stood shocked and speechless. Finally the doctor asked "Do you know what will happen if we let you go home?"

"I am fully aware of what I am demanding. You just need to tell me how long you think I have. We have lost the battle and it doesn't make any sense for me to go through any more torture. I am done." Rich wasn't angry or upset, he was just being matter-of-fact about everything.

The doctor did not want to answer Rich's question about how long. She said, "I will have your specialist answer those questions for you. You've made up your mind, I am convinced that you have all the information you need and you have proven yourself to be sane. We will certainly discharge you as soon as your specialist has approved it. I will get him here as soon as possible." She leaned over and put a compassionate hand on Rich's shoulder. "You know we are really going to miss you! Enjoy your days at home."

She had seen me move out of bed with Rich many times so they could do their visits with him. She knew how close we were. She looked across the bed at me, "How are you with all of this?"

"I'm fine. We've spent a lot of time talking about it and made the decision together. We know this is the end. We'll be fine."

We, too, would certainly miss the smiling faces and deep caring and warm friendships that we had developed with the doctors and nurses.

Within an hour the specialist came to visit with us. "Good morning. So, you want to go home! You don't want to try my big recipe? What information can I give you?" He was very careful to maintain his professional concern and compassion.

After Rich and I told him all that we had discussed amongst ourselves and the other doctor Rich asked, "How long do I have?"

"Well, after reviewing your numbers this morning I would say that if you keep taking all the oxygen, drugs and antibiotics you may live ten days to two weeks. If you stop taking just the antibiotics it would be a matter of days. No more than a week." He also told us the exact process the body would take right to the end. He gave us a moment to let the new numbers sink in. "What would you like to do?"

Rich replied, "Well, if the antibiotics can give me a few more days I guess I'll continue taking them."

"Ok then. I will get the order down to the pharmacy and have you discharged. The nurses will take care of the rest." He reached over to shake Rich's hand, putting his other hand on top. "I'm so sorry that I could not put you into remission!"

"Hey! You did everything humanly possible! If what you learned treating me can help you save a life later, that's all we can ask for Doc! You've been great!!"

Forcing a smile, the specialist said, "Thank you." patted Rich's hand and left the room.

"This is it! Are you still ok with all this?" Rich asked me.

"Like I said earlier; I am just so jealous that you get to go first. I want to be with Ray as bad and you! I'm the one that has to stay! Let's get the hell out of here.

224

CHAPTER FIFTY-FIVE

The nurse on duty came in to give us more particulars about the discharge process. She thought it would take a couple of hours. I left Rich so I could say goodbye to the patients and families I had gotten to know. We all cried a little, but each of us was there knowing that any one of us could be the one making the decision. We vowed to stay in touch.

I got back to Rich's room and began to gather up our belongings, making many trips down the elevator to the parking garage. Anna was excited about the commotion, but a little confused.

It was Friday, September 28th. Rich was ready to go. All I needed to do was stop by the pharmacy for the one week supply of meds. I had gone there earlier and they were putting together a full month's supply! NO!!! "ONE WEEK!!! "Only one week's supply please! If he needs more we will get them from our local pharmacist!"

As the hospital staff got him into the car, I ran back to the pharmacy with Anna. I gave them Rich's name, room number and the specialist's name. "Yes, we have them ready. That will be one thousand two hundred eighty-seven dollars and forty-nine cents."

"What!? Is it really that much for a one week supply?!"

"No, Miss. This is a one month supply."

"You are kidding!! Two and a half hours ago I asked that to be a one week supply! Why did it go back to one month?!" I was upset.

"I don't know. Let me check." He went away, returning to say, "I only see the order for one month. I'm sorry. Do you want us to re-do the order? I will need to call the doctor."

"NO!!! Never mind!! He's only expected to live a WEEK! What a WASTE!!!" I was not at all happy with the incompetency. I was shell-shocked about the cost! I was paying for drugs that I knew full well would have to be thrown away. That was quite a donation I was making to the pharmacy!

When I got to the car and loaded Anna, Rich was agitated. "What the hell took you so long?" When I told him what had happened he was even more upset. We both took a couple deep breaths and got on the road. Rich was pretty worn out from the discharge process. Neither of us knew how he would handle the four-hour drive, but he just wanted to be home so bad that his determination alone would get him through the discomfort.

We made only two stops, arriving home around seven p.m. I had called Jeff at the office that morning to let him know about our decision and what time we thought we would get home. If we had car trouble, he would be able to find us. Jeff said he would get the bed moved to the ground level so Rich would not have to go up or down any stairs.

A couple of my co-workers were there to greet us and help me get Rich into the house. He was able to walk, but just needed a little support. I was so grateful that they were there, but when I opened the door and walked into the house, I was even more grateful. The house was so clean and the bed was completely set up and ready for him to sleep in. It even had brand new sheets on it!

The hospital sent us home with two cylinders of oxygen. I worried that the oxygen would run out before the local company could get to our home. Because it was so late, I thought we would be lucky if the local oxygen company came on Saturday. I was wrong; they showed up after we had only been home an hour and by nine p.m. Rich was completely set up and all my fears about it were gone. We reviewed his medication schedule and made up a quick chart so I wouldn't forget any. He slept well and I slept well beside him—when I could.

Rich had called his brother when he made his decision to come home. It was a very emotional call for both of them. The days were now truly numbered for them, so his brother and his wife made the trip from Montana to see him for the last time.

They arrived fairly early in the day on Saturday. Nicki and I tried to let the brothers be alone together as much as possible. Rich was weak, but not weak enough to cut short the long conversations between them. I could sense the joy emanating from him while he was in the presence of his brother. The love bond was strong.

His brother left on Monday morning. Shortly after his departure, the hospice nurse arrived to set up end of life services. She was a wonderful person. All three of us talked about things we had been contemplating.

In the evenings or when Rich just needed to lay in bed, I would lie next to him and read to him from a book about the other side. Its title was "There Is No Death" written by Sarah LaNelle Menet. On Monday night, I had gotten to the part about the Silver Lake. This body of water that she describes glistens like diamonds and appeared like liquid silver. The water was as pure as pure could be. It was tranquil and inviting, yet seemed to have a life of its own. This lake is part of what she sees on the other side; what I refer to as Heaven.

Rich had been slipping in and out of consciousness while I read. I softly touched his shoulder and asked "Rich? Did you hear that part? About the Silver Lake?"

He didn't open his eyes as he replied to me "Yes I did. I know all about it. I've been there."

Since his brother had left, I could see Rich getting weaker. He had not only visited with his brother; we had several other visitors, including the priest from the local Catholic Church. Our dear friend across the street asked Rich if he wanted a visit from him. Rich was very thankful and gained peace from the priest's visit. Father said he was going out of town, but would touch base with us as soon as he returned.

Early Monday evening Rich received a call from Ron, his closest friend from Montana. He owned a truck repair and rebuilding business. Their business/customer relationship brought them together, personal friendship kept them close. As I listened to Rich's side of the phone conversation I heard him say, "No, No. You don't have to do that. I'm fine. I want to get out on my tractor tomorrow, and if I get some rest, I should be fine. Why don't you let me get back to you later in the week? Maybe you can make the trip during the weekend."

I knew that if Ron didn't make the trip immediately he would probably never see him again. Once Rich was finished talking, I saw him turn up the volume on the television and close his eyes. I grabbed the phone, ran up to the bedroom and dialed Ron's number. After my initial greeting I said "Ron, you know he is being overly optimistic."

"Shit, I know that! I just want to see him before . . . you know . . ." His voice was starting to crack and I could tell he was crying.

"Ron, you're his best friend. He isn't going to make it to the end of the week. If you want to see him you need to get down here NOW, not in three or four days."

"I'll be there tomorrow."

Rich and I had talked a lot about the fact that he had no fear of making the transition from mortal to immortal life, how he would

228

look after me from the other side and how he would give me signs so I would know that he was still with me.

During the night Monday I could tell he was fading. I continued to read the book to him even though he no longer acknowledged me and gave little response when I placed pills in his mouth. By Tuesday morning, I could no longer make him swallow a pill; even when I had crushed it and mixed it in a tiny bit of applesauce. It was as if he were falling into a deep sleep.

Between eight-thirty and nine a.m. Ron knocked on the door. Rich was lying nearly lifeless in bed, oblivious to the world. Unexpectedly, he opened his eyes to see Ron standing at his side. His face lit up like a Christmas Tree. "Ron! What the hell are you doing here!? How the hell are ya?!!" His voice was strong and clear.

"I drove eight hours through the night to see you! I'm not going to let you die without seein' you again! I love you man!" Tears began to stream from both of them. The energy between them changed instantly from strong and robust to soft and subdued. I left the room so they could speak privately. After a few minutes I peeked down the stairs to see Rich lying lifeless again, Ron's right hand on Rich's arm; his left hand wiping tears away.

A few moments later Ron came upstairs, gave me a hug and cried just a little. "I will be here for you for anything you ever need. Don't you EVER hesitate to call me for anything! I gotta go girl! You call me and let me know how he's doing." And just like that he was gone. I went back down to be with Rich. I just lay on the bed beside him.

Approximately two hours later Rich suddenly stirred, saying, "I need to go the bathroom." His speech was weak and slurred.

I told him "No, just stay in bed. You aren't strong enough to walk and I can't hold you up. I called the nurse and she is bringing a porta potty. Please just wait."

He was too weak to speak, but he was just strong enough to get out of bed. He couldn't wait. Now he was too far from the bed or a chair for me to do anything but use all my strength to keep him balanced upright. His body evacuated right there. The excrement was black. I knew this meant that his body had been bleeding internally, and this was the final stage. He mumbled, trying to say something, indicating how horrified he was about going on the floor. "I can clean the carpet! It's fine. Don't worry about it."

I managed to pivot him into a side chair that was nearby after I used my toes to grab a towel and get it on the seat of the chair. This little struggle depleted every bit of energy he had in him. His whole body wanted to roll forward out of the chair. His head hung from his shoulders; chin pressed against his chest. This position restricted his breathing, so I lifted his chin with one hand.

As I held him in the chair I grabbed the phone and rapidly dialed the nurse's number. As soon as she answered, I explained my situation expressing that I had no idea just how long I could keep him supported as he was like a wet noodle.

Within fifteen minutes she was there to help me get him back into bed. She took his vitals. Turning to me she said "It's not going to be long now; just a matter of hours. Do you want me to stay?"

"No that's ok. I want to be alone with him."

She had given me tips on how to clean the blood from the carpet, so as soon as she left I called the office and asked if one of them could pick up the items and could help me clean the mess. Two of them showed up ready to help with anything I needed. It was now about 12:30.

By 1:30 other friends from work stopped by on their way back to the office from a meeting. As we were visiting I noticed that Rich's breathing had changed. I asked them to leave. "Oh boy, this is it! I need you to go."

As they went out the door, I was dialing the phone number of the meditation/spiritual counselor. She had earlier agreed to help him cross over. Now was the time. Lying next to him, I held the phone to his ear as she explained what she was doing and what she would do as soon as she hung up. He replied to her questions, "OK. Good. OK." His voice was weak but clear.

When she was done speaking to him, I thanked her. She said there was no way she could tell me how long it would take for him to actually cross over. It was completely up to him.

He took his last, final breath fifteen minutes later. It was Tuesday, October 3rd.

CHAPTER FIFTY-SIX

Rich's funeral service was held on Saturday with the viewing the night before. As he wished, his body was cremated and again, I took the urn home. I now had three urns holding my boys: my husband and my two sons.

Rich's niece came to stay with me, arriving the day before the funeral. She was a great comfort and companion during the coming weeks. She witnessed all my mood swings. She helped me sort through and eliminate unneeded items.

I continued appointments with the grief counselor. We touched on my returning to work, but even after one month I was not ready to tackle the stress of work. I felt very weak; physically and emotionally. The pain of losing Ray had now been compounded by the loss of my husband. I was alone. I was a widow, no longer a mother, and my father and brothers were not talking to me. I felt like an orphan. I had no husband, children or family.

My boss had been a great friend the past thirteen years. We talked often after work over the years. Those conversations usually started with a business problem and then transformed into friend, family or child issues. We spent countless hours discussing morals and assisted each other in reaching solutions to dilemmas. He was my greatest source of support during all of my losses in the past year. I could always be straightforward and tell him exactly what was going through my head.

So here it was November, and I was still not working. I desperately needed some "talk-time" with Jeff. I certainly could have gone to the office to talk to him during business hours, but I knew that everyone there was doing their own jobs in addition to picking up everything I was supposed to be contributing. I purposely stayed away from the office.

Jeff and I continued to talk on the phone every few days. He knew that I needed some uninterrupted time for conversation so finally he stopped by the house and proposed that we go to a cabin in the Sun Valley area. "We" did not mean just him and me. He wanted Rich's niece, my neighbor and her granddaughter to join us. There would be plenty of time for us to talk there without business interruptions or pressures. The coming weekend was the President's Day holiday. We would have three days because the office would be closed on Monday. I welcomed the opportunity to spend time in different surroundings. The others joined us. Jeff, my niece and I went up together the evening of Friday, the tenth. My neighbor and her granddaughter joined us on the eleventh.

On Sunday, November 12th, after almost two days of talking, Jeff asked me if there was any way I could think of him as anything other than my boss. There we were, staring into the night sky from the therapeutic water in the hot tub. Our exposed wet hair was frozen, but our bodies were warmly wrapped in the water. His question came from left field; totally unexpected for me. I had no idea that he ever felt that way about me. I didn't hesitate to say yes. He had gotten divorced three years earlier, and I thought he still had a girlfriend. He told me of his concerns regarding that relationship but withheld much of it; spending his time listening to and supporting me. He was ready to terminate that relationship if I said yes.

Rich had only been gone six weeks. If any other person on the face of this earth would have asked me the same question, my answer would have been a resounding "NO." Jeff and I had been friends for thirteen years. We had total trust in one another. I knew well that if he said he would do something he did it, and that he would never see two women at once. He was taking a huge risk even asking me. If I said "no" he knew that our professional relationship, and possibly our entire friendship, would be over. He already knew exactly how I felt about anyone that "two-timed" on another, so I knew his query was serious.

The next morning we shared the news with the others. Rich's niece was very candid about what she thought. We had her full support. My neighbor was thrilled that he and I were going to be more than just friends. She had been my confidante for many years. She knew me well and also gave us her blessing.

Adding this new adventure to my emotional mountain was not exactly great timing. When I got home I found that I could not sleep, my body vibrated and it was difficult for me to stand. I was very frightened. What was happening to me? Was I disintegrating? I called my counselor.

"Sweetie, your mind and body do not have a clue how to react to something positive. That's why you are shaking and 'vibrating.' It is definitely too early to begin a new relationship, but from what you have told me through all our sessions, I trust your judgment. This physical response will subside. Just give it a little time. You are having something good happen . . . let it happen."

CHAPTER FIFTY-SEVEN

On November 19th, Anna came to the back deck after only being outside for about 15 minutes. Her body language and the look in her eyes told me something was wrong. Suddenly I could see why. Her front right shoulder was bleeding! Oh, my God. She'd been shot!! I had heard a neighbor across the street fire a gun, but at the time I heard the shot I just cursed him. He always shot the birds on his property, seldom considering what might lie beyond his target. Just the summer before, one of his bullets whizzed past me as I tended my garden. The only animal he liked was bovine. He loved his cows but nothing else. Now Anna was his victim. She came in and collapsed at my feet. Oh no! Not Anna! Not another death!

I quickly called the vet, who just happened to take the call himself instead of having his answering service pick it up. He told me to just load her up and get her to his office. He would get there at about the same time as me.

Anna was still alive, but could no longer walk. I don't know how I did it, but I carried her to the car. As I placed her behind the driver's seat I could see her eyes had opened as wide as they could get. "Don't you die on me! You hang in there until Dr. Bob can help you!!"

Rich's niece jumped in the car with me. As soon as I was out of the driveway I called Jeff. There was no way I could go through this alone. I needed him there. He would be there in ten minutes. My niece kept an eye on Anna as I drove to the vet's office.

As soon as we pulled up to the front door, Dr. Bob came out. Taking a look at her, he turned to me and said, "I don't know if she's gonna make it. Let's get her inside and see if there's anything I can do for her." He had obviously called his assistant because she was inside getting the x-ray room and other emergency equipment ready.

My mind was stable but my body was beginning to shake. The doctor did his work, giving her a shot that would help ease the shock she had gone into. He checked to see if the bullet had pierced her heart. No, thank God! Then he did an x-ray. She had been shot with buckshot. She had pellets throughout her chest area. He could see that she had a few in her lungs, but most were in the surrounding area. Somehow not one of the pellets hit her heart. He sedated her and took out the few pellets that were near the surface. It would be too dangerous to try to remove the others. As long as she came out of the sedative okay, she should be all right.

I was seething with anger at my neighbor, and in front of witnesses I used terrible language and made threats that no human should make. How could he do this to me!? He was well aware of my losses! How could he try to kill the only thing I had left?!!

Anna did make it through and recovered from her attempted murder. She is still with me today; happy and as healthy as I can keep her.

Jeff and I dated until the end of January. Then I gradually moved in with him, leaving my house to my niece until it sold.

Two years later, I finally felt ready to make a life commitment to Jeff. We married on November 12th, exactly two years after he asked me to be part of his life. "I Do."

POSTSCRIPT

There are no two ways about it. Losing the ones we love so dearly has to be the most difficult task God asks us to get through while we are living mortals here on earth. It becomes the true test of our emotional and spiritual strength. While seeing the grief counselor I expressed my journey this way: I feel like I was body-slammed off my bicycle, all banged up and dirty on the ground. I then decided to get up, go to the bike, pick it up and begin to push it. It hurts to push. It hurts to walk. It hurts to breathe. Gradually the dirt begins to fall off of me and pushing the bike isn't quite so difficult. Then I take the next step – getting back on the bike. That's a big step. I'm weak and the bike wobbles but I am moving forward. Slowly and gradually I am able to peddle with more confidence.

My personal spiritual evolution has saved me from the darkness. My life felt like all that Hell has to offer. I not only had to lick my wounds, but I also had to find spiritual support that made sense to me. Reaching out so many times and finding no salve for my wounds was disappointing at best. But I kept reaching out, reading, asking and listening to the answers until I found what worked for me. My job was to get out of Hell and it has been such a long and arduous endeavor. I am nowhere near finished but I feel like I have some control now.

I learned the art of meditation and how to use the intuitive skills that we all possess. I accepted the idea of intuitive/psychic readings and found that astrology readings can also assist greatly in understanding my life path. I have been blessed with highly-trained God-connected professionals. Finding spiritual guidance that I was comfortable with and trusted made the difference for me. After all this time I can finally say that Yes, I DID find the magic wand. I just didn't know I was holding it.

I have come to believe that we all are here on earth to complete challenges that we agreed to prior to being born. We made a contract with God and our Spirit Guides to do our best. We are given opportunities to go back to God. For me, those times were giving birth to Ray and hanging in the car over the cliff. While it appears that one person's challenge may not be as intense as someone else's, I believe that our spirits evolve and we will only choose those challenges that bring us to the edge – whatever that is. Once we are done as a mortal being we do indeed answer to God, but not to be judged so much as to go over the positives and negatives of our time away from Heaven. Everyone that we are in contact with while mortal has also made a contract with us to be involved in our life. Whether it be for 5 seconds or 50 years. It's ok that someone is only meant to walk with us for a short time. Do we have choices? Of course.

Having the freedom to choose was something that took me a long time to accept. I always thought our life was written in stone and we had no opportunity for variance. If we don't have choices, how then do we explain times when we make a decision and have to live with a complicated life for a period of time? It always seems to work itself out when we rely on the Supreme Being and his team of helpers. And when that time has passed we will always come away a bit wiser. A lot of people refer to those helpers as Angels. I find my comfort level with the term Spirit Guides. Do those who have passed before us contact us? Of course. How else can we explain those vivid dreams that make us feel so good or leave us wondering what the heck was that all about? Or for me – how could I explain finding pink guitar picks everywhere for months and months? Ray was leaving me gifts. No matter what mood I was in or how sad I was, the moment my eyes lit on the bright pink pick I couldn't help but smile. Yes, I could even smile through tears.

As Ray left me pink guitar picks and appeared in dreams, Rich also made his presence known to me. Rich first appeared to me in my dreams one week after his death. He had only been gone three weeks when I woke from a dream so real that I had to get up and get a drink of water to prove to myself that I was indeed awake. Rich had been spooning with me, just as we had all those years before. My skin was warmer where his body pressed against mine and I could still feel his breath on the back of my neck.

As soon as he passed on I began wearing the cross that he wore during his leukemia treatments. The cross was added to the broken heart charm on the rose-gold chain around my neck that I had purchased after Ray's passing. On one occasion I was discussing selling the old blue truck with Jeff as we drove down the road. A long-time friend and co-worker of Rich's had shown interest in it years earlier so I was planning on giving him a call. As I spoke the cross fell from the chain onto my lap. My jaw dropped. I grabbed the chain worried that it had suddenly broken and afraid that I had lost the heart charm. The chain and charm were still there, fully intact. Only the cross had removed itself from the chain. I could feel his presence and took the falling cross as an affirmation that I was doing the right thing. Rich's cross performed several "magic tricks" over the next twelve to eighteen months. After Ray's "gifts of presence" I was always ready and eagerly waiting to acknowledge Rich's next visit. Sad, but soothing moments in time.

Writing this book has taken me five years. Writing was *part* of my healing process. As I stated in my story, there were weeks and months where I could not emotionally bear to go into an empty room or deal with anything left behind by my family. That has been the case with most of Ray's belongings. I managed to deal with them enough to put them into storage when I sold my house but those things have been left untouched until now. As I prepare this manuscript for the publisher it is now six years after his passing and just now I find that I can retrieve one or two boxes from storage. As I sort through the toys, the Boy Scout badges and pictures, the school drawings and writing assignments describing family events I can *finally* handle those items without crying. I feel melancholy as I reflect back, but at long last I can look at those moments as a time past. It was a good life. Those were fun times, but that was my past life. I must live in *today* not yesterday. Yesterday was good, but so is today. Writing and sharing has done what I hoped it would—it has helped me move forward, leaving the largest portion of the emotion behind me instead of carrying it with me.

May sharing my life with you bring you strength and courage to move forward —even when the mountain before you appears impossible to climb. When you don't know which way to go, look down. Look at your feet. They don't point backwards. There's only one way to go. No one says you have to go fast. It's ok to go slow. It's ok to search for answers on your way.

I will leave you with two poems. I received one as a Christmas gift, written by my niece the year that Rich died. The other came from my Astrologer.

COURAGE

She sits on the riverbank,
Watches the water move with its old world magic
Listens to the peaceful lullaby that promises to bring hope
Feels the wind wrap around her like a warm embrace

She weeps
She screams

Her mind begins to take that long painful journey
To a time where there was no pain
She remembers their faces
She can hear their laughter
She can feel their embrace

She weeps
She screams

The pain rips her in two
The memories seem like dreams unfulfilled
Anger boils inside her
Sadness makes her numb to the world
She demands explanations from a silent environment

She weeps
She screams

Tears of a million questions blur her vision
As she struggles to see an image
It is small

She wipes the tears of past pain from her eyes to see
It is a flower ever moving and ever changing
It struggles to stay above
It fights to show the world its beauty, its mystery

She sees
She understands

As she watches this journey
She realizes the untold truths
She knows what she must do
Like the small flower she must have the courage to go on

She sees
She understands

By: Marie Moore

MY LAW   TIEME RANAPIRI

The sun may be clouded, yet ever the sun
Will sweep on its course till the Cycle is run.
And when into chaos the system is hurled
Again shall the Builder reshape a new world.

Your path may be clouded, uncertain your goal;
Move on--for your orbit is fixed to your soul.
And though it may lead into darkness of night
The torch of the Builder shall give it new light.

You were. You will be! Know this while you are;
Your spirit has traveled both long and afar.
It came from the Source, to the source it returns--
The Spark which was lighted eternally burns.

It slept in a jewel. It leapt in a wave.
It roamed in the forest. It rose from the grave.
It took on strange garbs for long eons of years
And now in the soul of yourself It appears.

From body to body your spirit speeds on
It seeks a new form when the old one has gone
And the form that it finds is the fabric you wrought
On the loom of the Mind from the fibre of Thought.
As dew is drawn upwards, in rain to descend
Your thoughts drift away and in Destiny blend.
You cannot escape them, for petty or great,
Or evil or noble, they fashion your Fate.

SOMEWHERE on some planet, sometime and somehow
Your life will reflect your thoughts of your Now.
My law is unerring, no blood can atone--
The structure you built you will live in--alone.
From cycle to cycle, through time and through space
Your lives with your longings will ever keep pace
And all that you ask for, and all you desire
Must come at your bidding, as flame out of fire.

Once list' to that Voice and all tumult is done--
Your life is the Life of the Infinite One.
In the hurrying race you are conscious of pause
With love for the purpose, and love for the Cause.

You are your own Devil, you are your own God
You fashioned the paths your footsteps have trod.
And no one can save you from Error or Sin
Until you have hark'd to the Spirit within.

Attributed to a Maori.
(Author Unknown)

ACKNOWLEDGEMENTS:

This book became a reality when Rosemary Sneeringer, my friend, meditation/intuition classmate and editor contacted me when she started a new editing business. She had offered to be my editor during our time in class years earlier, but little did I know then that she was the one who had been chosen for me until the day I got her email. Rosemary, you are the BEST! You were able to organize my "puzzle." Your sensitivity and ability to help me move through the tough stuff was magical.

Telling my life story has been one form of therapy. It has taken much strength to work through many of the emotional issues connected with it. It has been part of my healing process.

To my family members, thank you for being you. Your time in my life has been and will continue to be priceless. To Mom – Thanks for opening my eyes to the world of music and laughter, as well as responsibility. You have to be SO happy on the other side.

Rich and Ray, I miss you so much. Thank you for spending those years with me. I will honor you both the rest of my days as a mortal being.

I can never thank every single person who has touched my life. Many times I have spoken the words but many *more* times I had no idea that the contact would leave such an impression. Thank you each and every one of you. Your smile, twinkle in your eye, hug, your wave as you passed, your gentle hand on my shoulder or back, I hope to never forget. Your prayers and the strength you loaned to me for that fleeting moment helped me to take that next step. I am forever grateful.

Special thanks to my dear friends. You know who you are. Linda, you introduced me to Rich and have been there for me all these years. Your support has never waivered. Thank you.

And to every person who took the time to listen when I had to talk, and talk and talk – God Bless You! And to each of you who said "You should write a book and talk to people about it," you always delivered the encouragement I needed with impeccable timing!

To my husband, you have always been my friend, you are my beloved. Your endless love, support and encouragement has kept me going. Thank you for asking me to be part of your life.

All honor and respect I give to my meditation/ intuition teacher and Spiritual Counselor, Lisa Flores of Sacred Sun Healing. Your support and method of teaching has allowed me to take every step necessary to move forward. The skills I learned from you allow me live my life in joy.

And finally, my heart lies in the hands of the Supreme Being. Without you I would be no one. Without your love and protection I would have crumbled into nothingness. I rely on you every moment of every day. I trust that all is well with me this day and every day-- forever.

FREE MY HEART
OF GRIEF
TO LOVE

A JOURNEY FROM
LOSS TO JOY

A life worth sharing.

To have Sandra book a speaking engagement, or to find out more about the book, visit the website below.

www.sandrabernsen.com